A Gunner's Crusade

A Gunner's Crusade

The Campaign in the Desert,
Palestine & Syria as Experienced by
the Honourable Artillery Company
During the Great War

Antony Bluett

LEONAUR

A Gunner's Crusade: the Campaign in the Desert, Palestine & Syria as Experienced by the Honourable Artillery Company During the Great War
by Antony Bluett

Published by Leonaur Ltd

ISBN: 978-1-84677-382-2 (hardcover)
ISBN: 978-1-84677-381-5 (softcover)

http://www.leonaur.com

Publisher's Note

The opinions expressed in this book are those of the author
and are not necessarily those of the publisher.

Contents

To

My Wife

Foreword

Little has been said, and less written, of the campaigns in Egypt and Palestine. This book is an attempt to give those interested some idea of the work and play and, occasionally, the sufferings of the Egyptian Expeditionary Force, from the time of its inception to the Armistice. Severely technical details have been reduced to a minimum, the story being rather of men than matters; but such necessary figures and other data of which I had not personal knowledge, have been taken from the official dispatches and from the notes of eye-witnesses.

Here I should like most cordially to thank the following old comrades for their generous help: Capt. B. T. Hinchley, R.A.S.C., late of the Egyptian Camel Transport Corps, and L. Allard Stonard, Esq., late of "A" Battery, the Honourable Artillery Company, for permission to print their excellent photographs, which will, I am sure, add materially to the interest of the book; and R. Arrowsmith, Esq., late of "A" Battery, the Honourable Artillery Company, whose admirable notes have been of the greatest assistance to me in compiling some of the later chapters.

Antony Bluett
Highate, July 1919

CHAPTER 1

Mersa Matruh and the Senussi

It is a little difficult to know the precise place at which to begin this narrative. There are, as it were, several *points d'appui*. One might describe the outward voyage, in a troopship packed to three or four times its normal peace-time capacity; where men slept on the floors, on mess-tables, and in hammocks so closely slung that once you were in it was literally impossible to get out until the whole row was ready to move; and where we were given food (!) cooked and served under conditions so revolting as to turn the stomach at the bare sight of it. And there were other things....

But I do not think any useful purpose would be served by such a course. It was an unspeakably horrible voyage, but most of the troops travelling East experienced the same conditions; moreover, the praise or blame for those responsible for the early chaos will doubtless be meted out at the proper time and in the proper place. Again, as far as most people at home are concerned, the Great Crusade began with the taking of Jerusalem and ended when the Turks finally surrendered in the autumn of 1918. This view, entirely erroneous though it be, is not unreasonable, for a thick veil shrouded the doings of the army in Egypt in the early days, and the people at home saw only the splendid results of two years' arduous preparation and self-sacrifice.

Now the tale of these weary months ought to be told that

justice be done to some of the biggest-hearted men who ever left the shores of Great Britain and Australasia, and that the stupendous difficulties confronting them may be properly appreciated. It is no tale of glamour and romance; it is a tale of sheer, hard graft, generally under terrible conditions—for a white man.

Before we could even think of moving eastwards towards Palestine we had to set our own house in order. Egypt was seething with sedition, and the flame of discontent was sedulously fanned by the young excitables from Al Azhar, who probably were themselves stimulated by Turko-German propaganda—and "baksheesh." These had to be suppressed; and the task was not easy. Further, as far south as Aden there were Turkish garrisons, and troops in considerable numbers had to be detached to overcome them; this, too, was no small undertaking. Finally, a flowery gentleman called the High Sheikh or the Grand Sheikh of the Senussi had ideas above his station—and he had to be disillusioned.

This was a more serious matter, for the Senussi were the largest native tribe in Egypt, and Turkish and German officers had been very busy amongst them. Some account of the operations against them has already been published, but I believe it concerns mainly the Duke of Westminster's spirited dash with his armoured cars to rescue the shipwrecked survivors of the Tara, who were grossly ill-treated by the Senussi. Yet right up to the end of 1917 they were a source of trouble, and in 1915 the situation became so serious that a strong punitive force had to be sent to Mersa Matruh, on the Western Frontier of Egypt, to cope with it.

Here, I think, is where we must make our bow, for we had some small place in these operations; it was, in fact, our introduction to actual fighting, though we had already spent many torrid weeks on the Suez Canal. And no better *mise en scène* could we have than the old *Missa*, for the story of the campaign would be incomplete without mention of her; she was unique. Besides, everybody in Egypt knows the *Missa*. Those who had the misfortune to know her intimately speak of her with revilings and cast slurs upon her parentage.

Far back down the ages, possibly about the time when the admirable Mr. Stephenson was busy practising with his locomotive, the *Missa* might have been a respectable ship, but her engines had been replaced so many times by others more pernicious and evil-smelling, and new boards had been nailed so frequently and promiscuously about the hull, that she resembled nothing so much as an aged female of indifferent repute decked in juvenile and unseemly clothes; and her conduct matched her looks.

Most men in the army will have noticed that the authorities nearly always order a move or begin a "show" on the day of rest. I am no statistician, but if the tally of these lost hours in bed of a Sunday morning were kept, the army would have a few weeks' arrears of sleep to make up. On this particular occasion we went one better than Sunday; we began on a day when normally peace and goodwill go ringing round the world: Christmas Day, 1915. If there was any peace and goodwill about we failed to notice it, for it was blowing and raining hard, and we had to get half a battery of horse-artillery on board that deplorable ship.

It is no joke at the best of times embarking horses and mules; and as, in addition to the weather, we had the *Missa* to deal with, the humour of the proceedings did not strike any one—except the onlookers. For she rolled and pitched and plunged and dived as she lay there at her moorings. She was never still a moment, and, in a word, behaved like the graceless, mercurial baggage she was. But she was beaten in the end.

By dint of that curious mixture of patience and profanity characteristic of the British soldier when doing a difficult job, horses and guns were at length safely stowed away. Just before we sailed an old salt on the quay kindly proffered the opinion that it would be dirty weather outside. He was right. If the old *Missa* had behaved badly in Gabbari docks, she was odious once we got out to sea. She did everything but stand on her head or capsize—and did indeed nearly accomplish both these feats.

Normally the journey from Alexandria to Mersa Matruh, whither we were bound, occupies about sixteen hours. On this occasion the *Missa* took five days! A few hours after we left harbour the pleasing discovery was made that some one had mislaid a large portion of the rations for the voyage, though by a fluke several crates of oranges had been put on board—in *lieu*, perhaps.

Not that the question of food interested any one very much just then, for by this time sea-sickness was taking its dreadful toll. Men were lying about the wave-washed decks too ill even to help themselves; indeed, the only thing possible was to seize the nearest firm object and hang on. Watering and feeding the horses was a horrible nightmare, but somehow it was done. The former was carried out by means of horse-buckets—an interminable business, interrupted at frequent intervals when the men were shaken and torn by awful bouts of sickness as they staggered or crawled along the foul, evil-smelling hold. Feeding was rather easier and quicker, for there was little to give the poor brutes, even had they wanted it. So it went on for four ghastly days.

On the fifth day, rations, water, and even those blessed oranges had almost given out, and to add to our joy the skipper, who was afterwards discovered to be a Bulgarian, had not the remotest notion of our whereabouts and lost his nerve completely. A big Australian actually did take the helm for a time and made a shot for the right direction. We had almost given up hope of reaching the land when, in a smother of foam and spray, there appeared a patrol-boat, the commander of which asked in his breezy naval way who we were and what the blazes we thought we were doing. On being informed he told us we were steering head-on for a minefield, and that if we wanted Mersa Matruh we must alter course a few points and we should be in before nightfall. Also, he added a few comments about our seamanship, but we were much too grateful to mind—besides, they really applied to the Bulgarian skipper.

It sounds rather like an anti-climax to say that we landed safely. True, men and horses were too apathetic and ill to care a great deal whether they were landed or no. Many felt the effects of that turbulent trip for weeks after, and certainly no one wished to renew acquaintance with the *Missa!* The only pleasing feature about the business was, if report be true, that the Bulgarian skipper died suddenly from a violent stoppage of the heart.

Those of us who expected to find a great camp seething with activity and alive with all the pomp and circumstance of war were disappointed to see a mere collection of tents scattered about promiscuously, as it were, within handy reach of the shore. Here and there were piles of timber, R.E. stores, and the beginning of the inevitable ration dump; it was, in fact, a typical advanced base in embryo. Nobody seemed more than mildly interested in our arrival, with the exception of a supply officer who was making agitated inquiries about a consignment of forty crates of oranges which he said should have been on board.

When we were sufficiently recovered to sit up and take notice of every-day matters again, we learnt that there had been some very heavy fighting during December, culminating in a fine show on Christmas Day and Boxing Day, when the Senussi, although they took full advantage of the extraordinarily difficult country, were trounced so severely that more fighting was unlikely for some weeks. Curiously enough, this cheerful news rather damped our enthusiasm. We had come expecting to find a large and exciting war on the beach waiting for us. Instead, we found battery-drills innumerable for the better training of our bodies and the edification of our minds. Also, there were fatigues, long and strenuous, which our souls abhorred. It is curious how the British soldier loathes the very word "fatigue." He will make the most ingenious excuses and discover that he has extraordinary and incurable diseases in order to dodge even the lightest. Possibly the authorities, who sometimes see more than they appear to, had this in mind when later they changed the word to "working-party." There is a more dignified sound about it, though I don't know that it made the work any more acceptable.

In the evening we forgathered in an aged marquee used as a canteen, and cultivated the acquaintance of our new comrades, the Australian Light Horse, of which splendid corps more in the proper place. They were an independent but friendly crowd. Indeed, the word "friendly" is not quite enough; the Army one "matey" expresses so much better our attitude towards each other, after the first tentative overtures had been made. And this "matey" feeling animated the whole campaign against the Senussi, to a greater degree, I think, than any other. Perhaps the conditions drew us closer together, for they were deplorable.

It rained all day and almost every day; tents were waterlogged and one moved about in a slough of sticky mud. We ate mud, we drank it in our tea, we slept in it, for our wardrobes had been left behind in Cairo. Harness-cleaning was another bugbear, but even that succumbed to the mud after a time; and as the weeks flew by and inspections, infallible finger-posts to a "scrap," became more frequent we knew that all was not in vain and that very soon we should have the chance of justifying the long, arduous days of preparation. And quite suddenly it came.

One evening in the canteen the whispered news—"straight from the horse's mouth"—was passed round that we should be in action in two days! It was laughed to scorn. How often had we heard that tale before! There had certainly been an inspection of field-dressings in the morning, which usually meant something, yet even that had been done before and nothing had come of it. We were frankly sceptical. However, this time the doubting Thomases were wrong, for the very next day we were roused at a depressingly early hour by the guard, who told us in a hoarse whisper that we were "for it."

We were sufficiently experienced in turning out to get the preliminaries over quickly and without the amazing chaos that usually attends the efforts of the beginner. It is indeed remarkable how soon one becomes accustomed to working in the dark. Breast collars seem to slide into their places and buckles and trace-hooks find their way into one's hands of their own volition. By sun-up we were well on our way across the desolate, dreary waste.

It was terribly heavy going, over fetlock-deep in mud, as hour after hour we toiled along. Beyond small bodies of cavalry dotted here and there on the desert, there did not appear to be any signs of a battle. Men were riding at ease, smoking and talking, when, almost unnoticeably, the plain became alive with soldiers. Infantry appeared from nowhere in particular, the cavalry seemed suddenly to have increased considerably in numbers and to be massing as if for a charge, and before we realised it, we were unlimbering the guns and the horses were struggling through the mud back to the wagon-lines. In a few seconds the roar of an explosion proclaimed that the guns were firing their first shots against an enemy, and presently over the wagon-lines came a persistent whining sound indicating that the enemy had a few remarks to make on his own account.

The Senussi of course had the advantage of ground, but fortunately for us they had only light field-pieces which did little damage. They made astonishingly good use of their machine-guns, however, and soon had the cavalry, who had made an impetuous charge, in difficulties. So serious did the situation become that a gun had to be swung round—and extremely difficult it was to move in the mud—until it was almost at right angles with its fellow, in order to prevent our being surrounded. For some hours the Senussi made desperate attempts to outflank us, and both cavalry and infantry suffered considerably, nor did the artillery have much time for rest and reflection, for at one stage in the proceedings they were firing over open sights—and as any artilleryman knows, when that happens the enemy is quite near enough. It is of course impossible for one to describe an action like this in detail or say exactly when the turning-point came. There was the general impression of the infantry at long last heaving themselves out of the mud and going forward in real earnest, of the cavalry on the flanks speeding the heels of the retreating Senussi horsemen, and of the artillery firing as fast as they could load at any target they could pick up.

The whole engagement seemed to last only a few minutes, yet the artillery alone had been firing steadily for some five hours. When it was all over we were rather astonished to find ourselves still alive, somewhat dazed with the excitement and noise and with the cantankerous whine of machine-gun bullets still in our ears. A violent desire for a smoke was the first real sensation, but that desire was not destined to be gratified for some time, for our troubles were only just beginning.

The sticky mud had completely beaten the horses and mules, which latter had made a very praiseworthy attempt to stampede earlier in the day, and almost all the vehicles had to be man-handled along. Rain was coming down in a pitiless downpour and we had to face the prospect of a bitterly cold night with neither blankets nor greatcoats, for everything had been left behind to enable us to travel as light as possible. The plight of the wounded was pitiable. There were practically no medical comforts for them, most of the transport being stuck in the mud a considerable distance away.

Some of the slightly wounded men rode on the gun-limbers, others with more serious hurts in such ambulances as had managed to get up, a few on camel-back, while the remainder were actually carried in stretchers by their unwounded comrades. That these men with their heavy loads ever managed to lift their feet out of the mud was a miracle. I do not know what system of reliefs was adopted, but by the time the wounded were safely brought in, a whole battalion must have taken its turn merely to carry its own few casualties.

It was a magnificent example of devotion and dogged fortitude; and withal, the outstanding feature of the whole affair was the incorrigible cheerfulness of everybody, rising superior to all discomforts.

It may be thought that undue prominence has been given to an affair which after all was one in which a few thousands only took part—little more than a skirmish, perhaps, judged by European standards. It has been done partly because this was the first time most of us had been under fire, but chiefly because the battle was so typical of many in the subsequent desert fighting.

As will be seen later, the cumulative effect of these minor victories was out of all proportion to the numbers engaged. Moreover, this particular action again rammed home the lesson that native guerrilla troops cannot hope to tackle with success, well-armed, well-disciplined white troops supported by artillery.

Well, we had been blooded—lightly, it is true—and we were ready for the next job. We had learnt one or two lessons, for no one goes into his first action and comes out exactly the same man. He is rather like the good, but young and untried cricketer nervously going in to bat. The bowler looks about seven feet high and the stumps seem absurdly large; but the moment he is in the crease the mist clears away from his eyes and he is ready to set about his business. So it is with war: it is the fear of showing fear that makes many a good man unhappy in his first action; until he finds that he is not there merely to be shot at but to do a little shooting on his own account. After that he has little time to think about himself; he is too busy.

A plethora of fatigues occupied the next few weeks. A column started on a sweeping drive towards Sollum, but for us, beyond dropping a few shells into a native village, there was no further artillery action. Life resolved itself into an affair of G.S. wagons and patrol-duty, which latter chiefly concerned the cavalry.

There were lines of communication to be formed, contact with the railhead at Dabaa to be established and maintained, which meant, amongst other things, a constant carting of telegraph-poles out to unlikely spots in the desert, and dumping them there for "Signals," who immediately decided they would like them taken somewhere else even more remote and inaccessible.

Then, too, we were almost our own A.S.C. In the first place stores had to be brought by boat from Alexandria to Mersa Matruh, and the harassed and long-suffering troops were told off as unloading parties. At rare intervals a consignment of canteen stores would arrive, on which occasions the unloading party would be at the beach bright and early; things get lost so easily.

There were some crates of oranges once....

Two things the authorities at the base never troubled to send: clothes and boots. Apparently they were under the impression that we had taken to troglodytic habits and required none. Almost every man wore a patch; not like the tiny, black ornament worn on the face by ladies in the old Corinthian days, but a large, comprehensive affair more or less securely sewn on the shirt or the seat of one's riding-breeches. The quartermaster-sergeant complained bitterly over a shortage of grain-sacks: the reason for it was walking about before his eyes all day long.

It was dreary work at best, however, with only these uninspiring and never-ending fatigues to occupy our time. Even our little social haven, the canteen, did not stay the urgent need for something more active. The appalling thought came that we had been dumped down in this lonely desolate spot and left there, utterly forgotten, like Kipling's "Lost Legion."

There came a day, however, when our fears were dispelled by an urgent order to trek back to Alexandria. Apparently the war had broken out in a fresh place, and there was work to be done after all. Whatever the reason, there was joy in the camp. Tents were quickly struck and incinerators soon were working double shifts, for it is astonishing how things accumulate, even in the desert. Moreover, the army insists—and rightly—that camps be left clean and free from rubbish.

Rations, forage and water were the chief things to be considered—or rather, the problem of packing them on to limbers and in wagons—for they had to last us to railhead, some days' march away. Officially, once a unit is on the move, it ceases to exist till it reaches the next place on the time-table; and if rations or water are lost in the desert you go hungry, and, worse still, thirsty, for there are no more to be had.

Most of those who took part in it will remember that trek when others are forgotten. Rations were short, forage was short, everything was short, especially the ropes by which the horse-buckets were lowered into the wells; which last remark perhaps needs explanation.

All journeys in the desert are regulated by the distances between wells, which may be twenty, thirty, and sometimes more miles apart. At some of them we found the old-fashioned "*shadouf*," or native pump, which, clumsy though it was, helped matters considerably.

Usually, however, we had to rely on horse-buckets, and it was any odds that our ropes were too short to reach the surface of the water. The experienced driver would take a rein to the well with him, for lengthening purposes if necessary, but often some unfortunate wight, having found his rope two or three inches too short, would be seen struggling to hold his thirsty horses with one hand while with the other he endeavoured to unfasten his belt to make up the extra inches.

It was a maddening business, this watering the horses. Poor brutes! They would come in after a long day's trek, on short rations, with often a twenty-four hours' thirst to quench, and then have to stand round a well and wait perhaps for hours!

Even the quietest of them began to fidget and strain at their head-ropes the moment they scented the water.

As for the mules, there was simply no holding them. On one occasion—it was after a forty-mile march—a mule, frantic with thirst, broke away from his owner, and in a desperate attempt to get to the water, fell headlong down the well! A crowd of infuriated soldiers, with drag-ropes and everything that wit of man could devise, laboured for hours to get him out, while their comrades, equally infuriated, held anything up to a dozen animals apiece and made strenuous efforts to prevent them from following his deplorable example.

But, if the watering difficulty was the worst of our troubles, the shortage of forage was almost as bad, for the meagre ration of grain was about as satisfying to the horses and mules as Alfred Lester's famous caraway seed was to him.

The mules were the worst; they were insatiable. They ate the head-ropes that fastened them to the horse-lines, and the incensed picket spent half the night chasing them and tying them up again with what was left of the rope. Fortunately we obtained chains at railhead, and as these were uneatable they turned their attention to the horse-blankets and ate them! Soon it was impossible to "rug-up" at night, for there was not enough rug left. We used as pillows the nose-bags containing the following day's grain, and many a time were awakened by a half-famished mule poking an inquisitive muzzle under our heads.

Our own personal worries mainly concerned washing and shaving. Water was much too precious to be used for such purposes, so the problem was easily solved; we did neither. And in any case we had little time. We were up and away before dawn, we trekked anything from twenty-five to thirty-five miles a day, and when we had attended to the needs of

Native Market at Mersa Matruh

the animals and had something to eat and drink ourselves, we were too tired to do anything but roll into the blankets and sleep until a disgruntled picket roused us for another day. Occasionally some sybarite would be seen using the remains of his evening tea as shaving-water and laboriously scraping a three days' growth of hair from his face; but he was the exception. We were a ragged, unwashed, unshaven crew—yet mighty cheery withal.

And so we came to Alexandria, where baths, new clothes and boots, and, best of all, a mail awaited us.

Chapter 2

Somewhere East of Suez...

If you look at the map of Egypt and follow the line of the Suez Canal to its southernmost point, then continue a little down the Eastern shores of the Gulf of Suez, you will see—if the map be a good one—the words *"Ayun Musa,"* which being interpreted mean: "The Wells of Moses."

Now let your finger continue its journey due east, pausing not for mountains nor yet rivers, and it will inevitably arrive at a spot the name of which is variously spelt Nekhl, Nakhl or Nukul.

Concentrate on this for a moment and you will see that in enemy hands it formed a very effective jumping-off place for an attack on the southern terminus of the most important commercial waterway in the world and a vital artery of the British Empire. Moreover, it was very difficult of attack, for it was defended by a range of exceedingly unpleasant and precipitous hills, the passes through which were held by the Turks. Hence the agitation of the authorities and the sudden importance of Ayun Musa as a defensive barrier to Suez. It was to this lonely spot that we were ordered to proceed with the least possible delay. Having collected all the stores and camp equipment we could lay hands on, and after the usual circus in entraining the horses, we started for Suez. Incidentally, this was the last time we boarded a train as a complete unit for more than two years.

With Suez the last vestige of green was left behind us, and turning south after crossing the canal we entered upon that vast desert trodden by the Israelites thousands of years ago when they fled from the persecuting hand of Pharaoh.

It is to be admitted that we failed to observe, till later, the undoubted grandeur of the scene, for we were mainly concerned with getting our guns and overloaded vehicles along. Time after time they sank almost up to the axle-trees in the heavy sand and time after time did the sweating horses pull them out and struggle on again. One G.S. wagon, laden till it resembled a pantechnicon, was soon in dire straits. Originally starting with a six-horse team it acquired on the journey first one extra pair, then another—with a spare man mounted on each of the off-horses—and finally arrived in camp at the gallop with twelve horses and eight drivers.

Nobody saw anything funny in it. When you are dog-tired, hungry, and, worse still, when you arrive after dark in a new camp, nothing short of a cold chisel can gouge humour out of anything. All you want is a large and satisfying meal, after which your blankets.

In the morning we found that our usual fate had overtaken us: we were again pioneers in a new land. There it was, just our allotted square on the map, as flat and bare as a billiard-table.

Yet the country was not unimpressive. A thousand yards away to our right were the tamarisks of Moses' Grove, the only spot of verdure in sight; far in our rear and to our left ran range upon range of low, even-topped hills of unimaginable barrenness, the approach to which lay over a vast plain, broken by innumerable smaller hills, grand in its utter desolation; and in front of us stretched a level, shimmering expanse of sand as far as the silvery ribbon of the Gulf of Suez, beyond which, and dominating the whole scene, the gaunt, black mass of Gebel Atakah (Mountain of Deliverance) thrust its mighty pinnacle into the sky.

Such was the place destined to be our home for six torrid months; and we had to transform it into a fortified camp! Small wonder that we quailed at the prospect of work more punishing than any we had yet known, for literally everything had to be done; we had what we managed to bring with us, and that was all.

There followed days of unremitting toil. We turned our attention to road-making and with bowed backs and blistered hands shovelled up half the desert and put it down somewhere else; the other half we put into sandbags and made gun pits of them. We dug places for the artificers, kitchens for the cooks, walled-in places for forage, and but for the timely arrival of a battalion of Indian infantry we should have dug the trenches round the camp; we were mercifully spared that, however.

By way of a change we dug holes: big holes, little holes, round holes, square holes, rectangular holes; holes for refuse; wide, deep holes for washing-pits; every kind of hole you can think of and many you can't.

We never discovered for what purpose most of these holes were dug, but we dug them; and as a special treat we were allowed to dig an extra big hole, lined and roofed with sand-bags, wherein to hide two hundred thousand rounds of S.A. ammunition lest the Turks in a moment of aberration should drop a bomb on it. All this in a temperature of over 100° in the shade at nine o'clock in the morning!

For summer was leaping towards us with giant strides, and it was one the like of which Egypt had not known for seventy-five years. Day by day the sun waxed stronger until work became a torture unspeakable and hardly to be borne. With the slightest exertion the perspiration ran in rivulets from face and finger-tips; clothes became saturated and clung like a glove to our dripping bodies; and if a man stood for a time in one place the sand around was sodden with his sweat. Then, too, we had the usual difficulty about drinking water, for there was none in the camp. The Wells of Moses, twelve in number, were brackish and only fit for the horses.

Consequently every drop had to be brought from the Quarantine Station, three miles away, on the shores of the Gulf of Suez; and twice daily did the water-cart plough a laborious way through the sand. I think it was the very worst water we ever had, all but undrinkable, in fact. It was so heavily chlorinated and nauseous that one drank it as medicine. It tasted the tea, it spoilt the lime-juice, and even the onions failed to disguise it in the daily stew.

Fortunately there was washing-water in abundance, as we quickly discovered in our digging operations. Two or three feet down the sand was quite moist, and if the hole was left for a time, brackish water percolated through in sufficient quantities for a bath. It was the daily custom, after evening-stables, to rush across to the washing-pits, peel off our saturated clothes and stand in pairs, back to back, while a comrade poured bucket after bucket of water over our perspiring bodies until we were cool enough to put on a change of clothes.

And how we revelled in it! It was one of the few alleviations of those torrid, arduous days. You who dwell in temperate climes, with water—hot and cold—at a hand's turn, will perhaps accuse me of labouring the point. I cannot help it; no words of mine can express what it meant to have that clean feeling just for an hour or two. It was ineffable luxury; it helped us to endure.

For there were other things to add to our daily burden.

You will doubtless remember the Plagues of Egypt.... At least three of these survived at Ayun Musa to harass, thousands of years later, unfortunate soldiers who were trying to win a war. We had lice, boils and blains, and flies—particularly and perpetually, flies.

The first-named were not so terrible, for as wood was fairly plentiful we soon made rough beds and thus kept our clothes and blankets off the sand.

The second and third caused the medical authorities in the

East more trouble and anxious experiment than all the other diseases put together.

The slightest scratch turned septic. It was the rule rather than the exception for units in the desert to have 50 per cent. of their strength under treatment for septic sores. There was no help for it; active service is a messy business at best. It was appallingly difficult to give adequate treatment. Sand would get into the wound; if it were cleansed and covered up, the dry, healing air of the desert had no chance; if it were left open the flies made a bivouac of it—and the result can be imagined!

There were men who were never without a bandage on some part of their person for months on end, and it was a common sight to see a man going about his daily work literally swathed in bandages. It was not until we had advanced well into Palestine, where there was fruit in abundance, that this plague diminished and was in some measure overcome.

But infinitely worse than any other was the plague of flies. When we arrived at Ayun Musa there was not a fly to be seen. Within a week you would have thought that all the flies in the universe had congregated about us. They were everywhere. Did you leave your tea uncovered for a minute the flies around you hastened to drown themselves in it! And as for jam! Successfully to eat a slice of bread and jam was a feat, and one requiring careful preparation. You had to make a tunnel of one hand, wave the required mouthful about with the other for a few seconds in order to disturb the flies on it, then pass it quickly through the tunnel and into the mouth before they could settle again. One man nailed a piece of mosquito-netting to the front of the mess table and with himself as the pole made a kind of tent, so as to eat his food in comfort.

But meal-times were among the minor evils; it was in the tents, during the hours when we could do no work, that we suffered most. Rest was impossible. The mere touch of clothing was almost unbearable in the heat, but it was better to swathe the head in a fly-net and roll a blanket round the outlying portions of the body, than to strip to the buff and lie exposed to the attacks of those damnable flies.

It is no light thing that sends a strong man into hysterics or drives one sobbing from his tent, to rush about the camp in a frenzy of wild rage. Yet the flies did this—and more; they were carriers of disease. Behind the clouds of flies lurked always the grim spectre of dysentery; and of all our troubles perhaps this is the best known to the people at home. The Mesopotamian Commission ventilated it so thoroughly that there is no need to pile on the agony here. One may say, however, that the sufferings of the men in Egypt from this terrible disease were, certainly in somewhat less degree, those of their comrades farther east. And we will let it go at that.

Meanwhile, what of the Turks? During the six weeks we spent putting the camp into a state of defence they kindly refrained from annoying us, and beyond an occasional encounter with our patrols and a false alarm or two, nothing occurred to disturb the even tenor of our digging. When we had finished this strenuous pursuit, every ten days or so flying columns were organised to look for them and, if possible, drive them out of their rocky fastnesses thirty miles away.

One of the few vulnerable points in these hills was the Raha Pass and incredibly difficult it was even to approach. The joys of trekking over the sandy desert we knew, the desert in the rainy season we knew, but they were as nothing compared with the rocky desert of Sinai. Not only was there the deep sand to contend with but one had to climb hills and descend valleys covered with huge boulders. It was a creditable feat merely to get over the ground at all; manoeuvring was out of the question.

An eight-horse team could with difficulty pull a gun and its limber over fairly level ground; frequently twelve horses were required and sometimes as many as sixteen! And it was really wonderful to see them intelligently thrusting all their weight on the breast-collars, heaving and straining to get their load over a nasty place. These were the days, too, when the heat whipped off the rocks in waves and the sun's rays beat upon the back like strokes from a flail; when it was impossible to march during the noontide hours and one crawled under the limbers for shelter; and when a man looked longingly at his water-bottle, even though the water therein was almost boiling.

For the most part these flying columns drew blank. Rarely did the Turks and their Bedouin allies come out and fight, but confined themselves to sniping and harassing our cavalry-patrols at night. Every day these would return to camp bearing the body of a comrade, killed without seeing the hand that killed him; and once, saddest of all, two riderless horses, famished and almost mad with thirst, dashed up to the watering-troughs in camp. Their riders were never found.

We had to wait long weeks before our chance came. (Even then it came only just in time, for we left Ayun Musa for good the following day.)

It was rather a curious affair. The solution to the whole question lay in our being able to get the guns to the top of a certain hill commanding the Raha Pass. If this could be accomplished things would be very warm indeed for the people in the Pass.

It took twenty-six horses to pull the gun to the top of that hill! The rest was easy; almost too easy. The Turks had no heavy artillery, so we sat about in the open smoking and watching our guns shell them out of their holes into the arms of the Indian infantry, who went forward with a pleased smile to receive them.

But the urgent need in those days of the army in the East was aircraft; fast, modern machines, that is. There was a lamentable lack of anything that could go near the Fokker or Taube; the men were willing, but the machines were woefully weak. Almost with impunity the Turks came over and bombed the camps in the area; the one at El Shatt always received particular attention, possibly on account of its proximity to Suez, more probably because it was the largest and most strongly-fortified camp in the vicinity. Suez itself was attacked many times, as might have been expected, both on account of its immense oil-tanks and its position as the southern entrance to the Canal. Curiously enough, Turkish aircraft never troubled us much at Ayun Musa, though of course there was the usual "wind-up."

As a start we were ordered to convert our eighteen pounders into anti-aircraft guns. This meant digging pits with a weird kind of platform in the middle; this was for the reception of the gun-wheels alone. The trail was thus left free, which enabled the gun to be tilted sufficiently for high-angle fire. We never did fire at any aircraft from these pits; they looked very nice, however.

Nor did this finish the business. About this time the word "camouflage" appeared in the East and curiously enough, synchronising with its arrival, the mandate went forth that our tents were to be camouflaged. Now the army is a very wonderful place for teaching one to make bricks without straw, but if the other materials are lacking——?

Matters were at a deadlock till a bright lad suggested that there might be a little desert-scrub about if we looked for it. He was quite right; there was a little, a very little. About one bush to the half-mile was the average, and usually under a boulder at that. Every morning we rode forth and scoured the desert for that elusive scrub. As we had, by the process known in the army as "wangling," acquired sufficient tents and marquees for a battalion, there was a large quantity to find. Ultimately, after weeks of searching, we obtained enough, and to stimulate keenness, a prize was then offered for the best camouflaged tent. The winners' was really a very beautiful affair, but apparently the honour—or the scrub—was too much for the tent, for it collapsed during the night.

Shortly after this we had a further insight into the infinite possibilities of the desert. For a fortnight it had been intolerably hot, and rarely was the noon temperature below 120° in the shade. No work was done between the hours of 10 a.m. and 5 p.m., except at midday when the horses were watered and fed; and we loathed the whistle that summoned us from our tents into the blinding sunlight to perform this duty, necessary though we knew it to be. We literally prayed for the night and the cool breeze from the sea. The Mountain of Deliverance was in truth a symbol to us; for as we watched the sun sink slowly behind its sheltering bulk we knew that another day was done. We wondered wearily what this devastating heat could mean; it was like nothing in our experience.

One evening the whole sky was aflame with lurid light and we missed the revivifying breeze. In its place came a hot wind from the south-east, and although the sun was setting we could feel the sickly heat increasing momentarily. Presently, far over the eastern desert could be seen a gauzy cloud of immense size travelling towards us at a tremendous pace. In a few moments we were in the midst of an inferno of swirling sand and suffocating heat. It was the dreaded *khamseen*.

Men rushed blindly for their tents and swathed their heads in shirts or blankets in order to keep out as well as might be the flying particles of sand. Fortunately for us the high embankment in our rear protected the camp to some extent and we never got the full force of the sandstorm.

For three days it raged. Little work was possible beyond watering and feeding the horses. The short walk from the horse-lines to the watering-troughs was sheer torment, for the hot wind came down the slope like blasts from a furnace. It did literally turn the stomach. Many a man staggering blindly along with his three or four horses would pause, vomit violently and carry on. The horses neither drank nor ate much, poor brutes, but all day long stood dejectedly with drooping heads, their backs turned to the scorching wind.

It was a scarifying experience. When, on the evening of the third day, the familiar wind came up from the sea we had the feeling one has on coming out of a Turkish bath into the cooling-chamber.

Another welcome tonic was the news that the brigade was ordered to Salonica. We felt that any change would be for the better; in any case it could not well be worse. And so we fell to making our preparations with light hearts, confident that in a few days we should be on the move again, perhaps—who could say?—towards a real war. At the last moment a wire came cancelling the move. The disappointment was so bitter that it knocked all the life out of us for days. We felt like a boxer who, after a knock-down blow, rises at the count of nine, say, and is at once sent down again for good. The knock-out blow was that in our case the rest of the brigade did actually leave the camp, in addition to which the Indian infantry who had lain alongside us also went elsewhere. We felt thoroughly aggrieved.

I suppose every unit at some time or other during a period of enforced stagnation has had this grievance. Nobody loves you. You feel that some one in the high places has a grudge against you. You can hear him saying to his underlings: "Let me see. So-and-so is a pretty rotten camp, isn't it? I'll keep this battalion or that squadron or the other battery there. Do 'em good. Mustn't coddle 'em." And you are kept "there" for weary months.

Most of us knew that the conditions in Salonica were as bad as, if not worse than, those obtaining in Egypt, so why on earth were we pining to go there? There is no prize for the answer, but I suspect it was the eternal desire for a change, of whatever nature. Besides, except for the heat, flies, septic sores, the khamseen, bad water, dysentery, vaccination, inoculations many and various, digging holes, and a depressing sameness about the scenery, we had, according to some, little to grumble at.

We were not unduly harassed by the Turks; indeed, it was our function to harass them. We slept peacefully in our beds o' nights except for a pernicious system of false alarms. We had now a metre-gauge line on which our forage was brought into camp, thus saving us a fatigue. Moreover, on this line we could take an occasional joy-ride in a tram like an Irish jaunting-car, drawn by two mules probably also of Irish descent, who invariably ran away with the tram, and, desiring later to rest awhile, were as invariably thrust forward again by the violent impact from behind of the oncoming vehicle.

We had a very passable canteen with sometimes real beer in it. And above and beyond all these joys we had recently made an ice-chest. True, we were dependent upon a somewhat fortuitous supply of ice, brought by boat across the Gulf from Suez to the Quarantine Station, thence by special fatigue-party, armed to the teeth, into camp; and it usually suffered considerably en route. But think of a long, really cold drink waiting for you at the end of a three-days' stunt into those iniquitous hills, when you came in covered with sand and with a throat like a dust-bin! Half of it went at a gulp to wash the sand down; the rest one drank slowly and with infinite content. That ice-chest had the prestige of a joss.

Looking back, however, on the summer of 1916 and taking count, as it were, of the things that amused us and helped us to carry on, I find that we were for the most part self-supporting. To the best of my recollection, except for visits of inspection by the Great Ones, which of course do not count, there were only two occasions when we had strangers within our gates.

The first was when the navy, some forty strong, in high spirits and a G.S. wagon, came to cheer us up.

And here I should like to ask why it is that the moment the sailor man is ashore he goes forth and looks for a horse, quite regardless as to whether he has ever put a leg across one before or no. For them, too, a horse has but one pace: a full-stretch gallop. It took hours to catch all the riderless horses

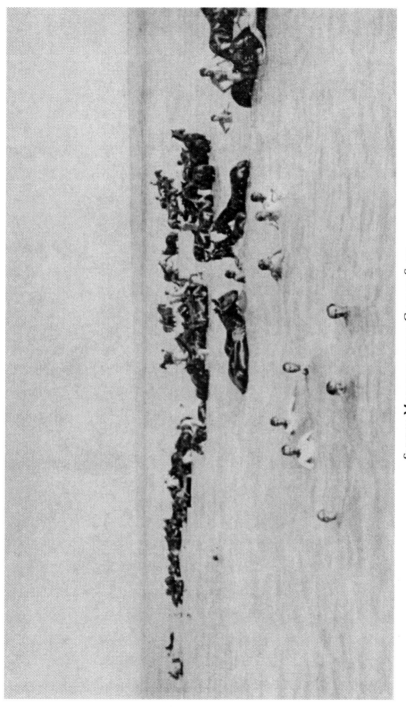

Sunday Morning in the Gulf of Suez

after the navy had started for their gentle exercise, but we got heaps of fun out of it and it was very good to see somebody from the outside world.

The other time was when we had a concert in Moses' Grove and a regimental band came from El Shatt to entertain us. It was fine to sit there under the tamarisks around an immense camp-fire and listen to a really good band playing the old favourites again and giving us a few new ones, to be whistled or sung about the camp for weeks.

The mail, of course, kept us happy where nothing else could, for not only was it the single link with home and all that it meant, but it brought us newspapers which, while carefully avoiding all reference to the armies in the East, did tell us of the war as they waged it in France. Also, it introduced Bairnsfather to us. "The Better 'Ole" became almost an institution; we could speak with authority on "'oles." And "When the 'ell's it goin' to be strawberry?" was the unfailing jest at meal-times, as we scraped the layer of flies from the top of the inevitable Tickler.

No doubt these things will strike you as trivial. Quite so. But when you remember our complete isolation, that for six months we saw no one but ourselves, so to speak, you will understand that if one did not laugh at trivial things one simply did not laugh at all—and in the desert that way madness lies.

For there were days when one hated the sight of one's best friend, when the mere sameness of everything drove one almost to distraction, and when the heat and the little exasperations of our daily work kept the temper constantly on edge. One had to laugh at something; it was the only way to keep sane. So, if there should occasionally creep into these pages a somewhat frivolous tone, I crave your indulgence, for it was truly the atmosphere in which we, in common with other lonely outposts, lived and worked. It was fatal to take life too seriously; wherefore, as we had little else to laugh at, we laughed at ourselves.

But to all things an end. The weary time of waiting and preparation was almost over. Sparse news filtered through that the northward advance towards Palestine had already begun; that there had been heavy fighting at Katia, where the Turks, under cover of a desert mist, surprised and cut up—but failed to defeat—our cavalry; and that we had at Romani inflicted the most summary defeat on the enemy since he made his abortive attack on the Canal in 1915.

All of which, said the wiseacres, seemed to point in one direction; that all the available troops would very soon be required for the more considerable business at the northern end of the desert; in other words, that we should shortly be on the move again. And for once the prophets were right, for suddenly there was a great to-do in the camp; such a polishing of guns and a burnishing of stirrup-irons and bits and chains, such a cleaning of harness and saddlery as had never been known.

When it was done one of the elect came down and inspected us, after which we went out into the desert beyond and fired at targets the ranges of which had been carefully taken days before, so as not to disappoint the great man by bad shooting. Whereupon, when he had expressed himself satisfied with the accuracy of our fire and the smartness of our drill, he went away; and presently came others, still more elect, for whom there was more cleaning and burnishing, and who further declared their entire approval. Finally the Commander-in-Chief himself came and inspected all the troops in the area; and the work was as before, only more so. Now, when he too was pleased, we knew that a move was what the Americans call a "cinch." And so it proved. To wind up with a flourish, as it were, we went out to the hills again for a last—and, as it happened, most successful—attempt on the Raha Pass, when we climbed the hill mentioned earlier in this chapter.

Marching orders were awaiting us on our return. We were to trek to El Kubri, a post on the Canal near Suez, there to await train accommodation. This time the orders were not cancelled.

CHAPTER 3

On 'Unitin'—and Some Other Matters

Having got us to El Kubri and told us to wait for a train, the authorities apparently washed their hands of the whole affair and forgot all about us. For six weeks we waited at a siding which seemed to be ashamed to look a train in the face. Certainly we never saw one approach it, and we kept a careful look-out for fear we should miss one.

On our arrival we did not, of course, make a camp, believing that we should entrain in a day or two at most. But as day followed day and no train appeared we began to think that this was a joke in deplorable taste. Why, after working for six months like niggers are supposed to work making a comfortable camp, should we be taken therefrom, dumped down on an inhospitable siding and forgotten? It was not playing the game; and a sinister rumour spread that we were not going north after all but were to be sent down the Red Sea to the assistance of the Cherif of Mecca, who was having a little war on his own account.

We knew what that meant. The assisting force would be sent to some evil-smelling native town with an unpronounceable name, miles from anywhere, left there to garrison the place and impress the inhabitants with the might of British arms, while the Cherif and his wild horsemen charged about the desert firing rifles in the air and emitting extraordinary yells to frighten away the few stray, half-starved Turks in the vicinity. And the prospect of travelling in a horse-boat down the Red Sea, even in November, did not appeal to us in the least. However, tired of sleeping in culverts and disused drains we pitched our camp on the top of a plateau overlooking the Canal and prepared to await developments.

It was not unpleasant waiting, for there was the daily bathe in the Canal, and the big ships and liners passing up and down seemed to bring us once more in touch with civilisation. It used to be the kindly practice of the passengers to throw tins of cigarettes and tobacco overboard whenever the boat passed one of the numerous outposts guarding the Canal. It was quite an ordinary occurrence for a man to dive in with all his clothes on and swim after the coveted tins. Tobacco was so scarce that a mere wetting was nothing; besides, our clothes were dry in an hour.

Also, we hunted the fox—or rather, jackal.

Now the Egyptian native undoubtedly looks on the British soldier as *magnoon*, afflicted of Allah, to be treated kindly, but to be relieved of as much of his hard-earned pay as possible. And further, if the Faithful are able to obtain something for nothing from these amiable madmen, it is to be done. So we made ourselves popular with the *fellaheen* by hunting jackals, which had the same predilection for other people's chickens as has brother fox in England.

We had no hounds, except a fox-terrier who was too fat to run; only our horses and our prodigious enthusiasm. The method of procedure was to assemble the hunt near a likely place and send forward a fatigue-party to dig out the jackal. When he appeared—and he usually did appear in a hurry—we gave him a couple of minutes' start and then tally-ho! and away after him over the plain. We had, of course, no fences to leap, but there were deep *nullahs* and irrigation dykes wide enough to give one something to think about. Moreover, the jackals were astonishingly speedy; they would twist and turn and double on their tracks for half an hour at a stretch, and they were game to the end.

Christmas came and was made endurable and even enjoyable by the kindness of the Y.M.C.A., who lent us tables, yea and cloths, in addition to other things.

But the outstanding event of this period of waiting was the visit of one of Miss Lena Ashwell's concert parties to El Kubri. It will ever remain a fragrant memory, for it was the first time we had seen English ladies for nearly a year and it brought home very near to hear them sing.

They gave their concert in a specially constructed "hall" in the desert. Sandbags were the mainstay of the platform and a large tarpaulin, G.S., formed the drop-scene. The walls were of rough canvas, upon which it was inadvisable to lean, lest the whole structure collapsed. Primitive, no doubt, but it suited the environment; and I have never seen in the most elaborate West-end theatre anything like the enthusiasm here.

You called for a popular song or recitation and you got it, and as many more as you liked to ask for. One of these talented ladies used to give a recitation which became a permanent feature of her programme in Egypt. She would come to the front of the stage and say confidentially to the audience, "Do you know Lizzie 'Arris?" And back would come a mighty bellow, "*Aiwa!*" This rite was always insisted upon before the artiste could proceed, though she obviously enjoyed it almost as much as we did. She might probably be amused to know that—such is fame!—amongst the thousands of troops who heard her recite she was always known as "Lizzie 'Arris."

Early in the New Year the Mecca myth was finally dissipated, for we moved—no, the train never arrived—to the big concentration camp at Suez, and there started preparations in real earnest. It was strange to be amongst people again after so many months of comparative solitude, and stranger still to see houses and streets and civilians. Not that we had much time to look around, for with the coming of the cool weather the hours of work became appreciably longer.

Every day long columns of infantry went forth to get themselves into hard condition by strenuous route marches. Dotted about the camp were little groups of specialists and others practising their several trades. Here was a bombing-school urgently killing imaginary Turks; there a squad of bay-onet-fighters engaged in the same pleasurable pursuit; while farther away an eager band of signallers with their handy little cable-wagons laid a wire at incredible speed.

Away out on the plain a string of harassed recruits trotted round a rough *manege* lustily encouraged to a rigid observ-ance of the good old maxim, "'eels an' 'ands low; 'eads an' 'earts 'igh," by the astonishing profanity of their riding-mas-ter; and beyond them their more proficient comrades charged with wild yells upon a long line of stuffed sacks representing a terror-stricken foe waiting patiently to be spitted.

Hard by these perspiring cavalrymen a battery of horse-artillery struggled to master the intricacies of driving with fourteen-horse teams. These were arranged in three rows of four abreast with one pair in lead, while of the drivers three rode the near-horses and three the off-horses, with one driver riding the near-horse of the leading-pair; a complicated busi-ness requiring much skill and nicety of judgment in order to get the best out of the horses.

Occasionally an apparently wild chaos of guns and limbers and horses proclaimed that the battery had been successfully brought into action; usually, however, the work was confined to getting the vehicles along under these novel conditions. Along-side our own, French artillery with their natty little "75's" daily strove to put the finishing touches to their preparation.

It was to the confines of the camp that one went for the final signs that a "show" was surely preparing, for here were all the dumps of material which was to minister to the needs of an army in the field.

Sacks of grain and bales of *tibbin* stood in huge pyramidal mounds; multitudinous rows of boxes containing bully-beef, condensed milk, dried fruit, biscuits, cocoa, and tea, seemed to stretch for miles. One walked down streets of bully-beef, as it were; loitered in squares bounded by biscuit-tins; dodged up alleys flanked by tea-chests and cases of "Ideal" milk. Through the streets and squares came an endless procession of lorries and G.S. wagons, passing on their lawful occasions.

After all, the final word rests with the A.S.C. All your preparation, all your study of new methods, all your concentrations of guns and men and horses are futile—and how futile!—if the Army Service Corps says: "Sorry, gentlemen, but we can't feed you; and if we could, there's nothing to carry the food in." In the beginning this was especially true of Egypt; for there was a lamentable shortage of nearly everything that goes to the successful waging of war. It took nearly two years of patient endeavour before an advance could really be considered, and by far the greater part of that time was devoted to amassing supplies and organising means of transport. It was a colossal task, the magnitude of which was never even imagined by the people at home.

There was practically nothing in the country. We wanted sleepers, rails, and locomotives for the railway; pipes, pumps, and other materials for the water-supply; wagons, motor-lorries and light-cars for transport purposes; sand-carts, *cacolets*, and ambulances for the R.A.M.C.; and, with the exception of most kinds of vegetables, food.

All this had to be brought overseas.

There may not at first sight seem to be any striking connection between an enemy submarine and the date of an offensive. When, however, that submarine torpedoes and sinks a vessel containing two million pounds' worth of absolutely essential material, such as locomotives or motor-lorries, the connection becomes less, as the date of an offensive becomes more, remote. In fact, as neither a locomotive nor a motor-lorry, nor a boat wherein to carry them can be built in five minutes, the offensive temporarily recedes from view, until the next boatload of material is safely landed.

Add to this the facts that a hundred and fifty miles of desert had to be cleared of an enemy who fought with the most bitter determination all the way, that a railway had to be constructed, and an adequate water-supply had to be maintained over the same desert, before an offensive on a large scale could even be dreamt about, and the connection mentioned above becomes strikingly obvious.

Those people at home who, from time to time, asked querulously, "What are we doing in Egypt?" should have seen Kantara in 1915, and then again towards the end of 1916. Failing that I would ask them, and also those kindly but myopic souls who said: "What a picnic you are having in Egypt!" to journey awhile with us through Kantara and across the desert of Northern Sinai. For the former there will be a convincing answer to their query; the latter will have an opportunity of revising their notions as to what really constitutes a picnic.

And we will start now, while the scent is hot, for already the infantry have begun their march and guns and wagons are rumbling along the roads from Suez to Kantara, the gate of the desert.

CHAPTER 4

Kantara and the Railway

At this point it would be as well to confer with the map once more. Be pleased to imagine that we have trekked northwards from Suez, through the beautiful little town of Ismailia, "the emerald of the desert," thence to Ferry Post, which was a position of considerable importance when the Turks attacked the Canal in February 1915, and finally to Kantara, where we will pause to see if an answer can be found to the query propounded in the preceding chapter.

If our inquiring friends had sailed down the Canal in 1915 they would have seen at Kantara—had they noticed the place at all, which is unlikely—a cluster of tents, a few rows of horse-lines, some camels, a white-walled mosque, and a water-tank close to the water's edge; while their nostrils would have been pungently assailed by the acrid smell of burning camel-dung.

It is at least probable that the last-named would have made the most striking impression. (It is still a powerful characteristic of Kantara.) Certainly they would never have guessed from its appearance what Kantara was destined to become: the terminus of the great military railway running across the desert and through Palestine, a military port of the utmost value, the beginning—or end—of the main road into Palestine, and the biggest base in Egypt.

They are to be excused; no one would. Kantara did not unduly lift its head in those days, and one did not, perhaps, at a first glance fully appreciate its unique geographical position; for it is situated within easy reach of Port Said and Suez, the two great termini of the Canal, and is thus conveniently near the sea.

Moreover, the Turks were only some fourteen miles away, and the time was not yet ripe. It is illustrative of our early limitations that our postal designation was "Mediterranean Expeditionary Force, Canal Defences." Note that no idea was then entertained of anything beyond defending the great waterway.

Nothing else could be done. We had simply to hold off the Turks and make shift as best we could, meanwhile collecting materials and making preparations for a definite offensive when the psychological moment arrived.

Originally the troops were on the west bank, near the station, which is on the State Railway from Port Said to Cairo and Alexandria, until some one high in authority suggested that as we were supposed to be defending the Canal, and not the Canal defending us, it would be as well to move over to the other side. The fact is, this would have been done much sooner had it not been that the Turkish attack in February caused what is called a vertical draught in political circles in Egypt, and it needed a very great man indeed to order the move.

We were still dependent on Port Said for rations and supplies, while all the water was brought up from the same place by boat and stored in the big tank. The means of communication between the east and west banks were somewhat primitive. At Kantara a pontoon bridge and a decrepit chain ferry of uncertain moods maintained irregular intercourse with the other side. It used to be one of our diversions to watch the ferry bringing across the daily ration-wagon, whereof the horses, frightened by the clank of the chains, frequently bolted the moment the "door" of the ferry was lowered. To the right, in the direction of the camp, was a particularly nasty incline, so the wagon usually decided to go to the left through the lines of the Bikanir Camel Corps; whereupon the horses, having an unconquerable aversion to camels, at once stampeded, and our rations were in dire jeopardy. There were, too, a few rowing-boats for passengers, but these were either on the other side when you wanted them or were too full of holes to use.

Patrol-duty and spy-hunting were our principal occupations, as in most of the other Canal stations; certainly few dreamed of the greatness in store. It was not until the spring of 1916 that Kantara dropped its mantle of obscurity and began to take its place as our principal base of operations. From then onwards the place hummed with ever-increasing activity, for the danger of a further attempt on the Canal was now somewhat remote, and work could be carried on in comparative safety.

One day, perhaps, a scribe will rise up and write of the doings of the Royal Engineers in this war, more particularly of their deeds in such places as Salonica, Mesopotamia, East Africa, and Egypt; where, in addition to the usual shortage of tools and material, they had to wrestle with every conceivable kind of geographical obstacle that a bountiful Nature could place in their way. The present scribe can only write of what they did in Egypt and Palestine, and not half of that can be told.

As far as Kantara is concerned they came, they saw, they conquered. What they saw was a desert which they proceeded to transform into a city, certainly of tents and huts, but "replete with every convenience"—as the house-agents say. As a start they pensioned off the aged chain ferry into decent retirement and built a goodly swing bridge, over which were brought timber to be cut into beams and joists; nuts and bolts and screws, and an *olla podrida* of materials.

When this was done a gentleman called the Assistant Director of Works came and made a plan of the city. Here a difficulty arose. In this climate a white man has his limitations, and one of them is that hard manual labour when the sun is summer-high is exhausting in the extreme, and is, moreover, explicitly forbidden between the hours of 10 a.m. and 4 p.m. by the authorities.

It was then that the voice of the Egyptian Labour Corps was heard in the land. Little is known outside the country of this admirable corps, yet it is scarcely too much to say that they saved the situation here as elsewhere. Recruited from almost every class of the native community, from the towns and cities, from the Delta, from their *belods* in the far-off Soudan, they came in thousands to dig and delve, to fetch and carry, to do a hundred things impossible for a white man to do in that climate. It is difficult to over-estimate their usefulness; though not as a rule big men, they would carry for considerable distances weights that a far bigger white man failed even to lift.

Their staple diet consisted of bread, onions, lentils, rice, dates, and oil—with perhaps a little meat after sunset. They drank prodigious quantities of water, and could not in fact go for long without. Firmly but fairly treated by their British officers and non-commissioned officers, they went anywhere and did anything; and wherever you found the sappers, there, too, you would see the khaki *galabeahs* and hear the eternal chant: *"Kam leila, kam yom?"* of the E.L.C. Under their hands Kantara took shape. Supervised and directed by the Engineers, gangs of them made roads, workmanlike affairs calculated to stand the strain shortly to be imposed on them by the daily passage of thousands of lorries and wagons. Eastward from the Canal what had been a mere track, fetlock deep in sand, became a broad road macadamised for ten kilos, from which radiated similar roads in all directions, and on which abutted presently the great camps that seemed to spring up like mushrooms in a night.

Alongside the roads other gangs laid water mains connected directly with Port Said, for it soon became utterly impossible to bring an adequate daily supply of water by boat. At certain points stand-pipes were erected so that working-parties and other troops could fill their water-bottles without having to go far to do so; in the hot weather every extra yard tells.

This was the beginning of the pipe-line laid stage by stage as the army advanced, across the desert and far into Palestine. We shall see more of it later.

Then the A.D.W. collected his carpenters and bricklayers and bade them instruct their dusky labourers in the building of gigantic mess-huts, in size and shape not unlike a hangar, capable of providing meal accommodation for hundreds of men at a time; ration and store-huts for the numerous camps; brick enclosures for the kitchens; incinerators, and a thousand and one things necessary for the troops. It was a liberal education to watch a British N.C.O. working with the gang of natives under his command. Usually his entire vocabulary of Arabic consisted of about ten words, of which the following are a fair sample:

Aiwa—Yes.
La—No.
Quais—Good.
Mush quais—No good.
Igri!—Quickly!
Imshi!—Clear out!
Ta-ala henna—Come here.

With these, comically interpolated with English expletives, he performed marvels, from stone-breaking to bridge-building.

Presumably he gave his instruction by some process of thought-transmission, an art that seems peculiarly suited to the genius of the British soldier. "*Quais!*" he would say, when a man had done a job to his liking, and the man's comrades crowded round carefully to examine the work, after which they went away and copied it faithfully. If on the other hand, the man failed to do what was required of him, there would be an aggrieved bellow of: "*La! Mush quais!*" and the perspiring native would get down to it once more, while the others charged up again to see what in future to avoid. Moreover, whatever mistakes they made subsequently it was rarely that one.

"*Igri*, Johnny!" or alternatively and more forcibly, "Get a

51

bloomin' *igri* on, Johnny!" was the favourite ejaculation of an
N.C.O. when he wanted to cure that tired feeling peculiar
to the Egyptian native. (All natives answer to the name of
Johnny, by the way.)

"*Imshi!*" was the N.C.O.'s great word, however; he used
it on all occasions implying a departure from his presence;
when a man's face displeased him, for instance, and when he
dismissed them for the day. They made a weird combination,
these two, the dominant white man and the dusky native; but
they built Kantara—and a few other places.

As the camp grew and grew so also did its needs. The Army
Service Corps arrived in force and demanded for themselves
a great depot, covering many acres, which was to be the Main
Supply of the army advancing into Palestine. Materials and
stores could not now be brought in sufficient quantities by
the State railway on the other bank, and the traffic over the
Canal bridges was becoming increasingly heavy. Accordingly
the engineers found another outlet for their energies: they
created a fleet!

Jetties and wharves were built on the east bank, and to
them came presently numbers of strange vessels, broad in the
beam like a barge, and with monstrous lateen sails that looked
too unwieldy to be furled or set; and on their bows they
bore the painted letters "I.W.T., R.E." and a numeral. They
were native feluccas, garnered from every canal and waterway in Egypt. They brought grain and fodder for the horses,
rations for the men, vegetables of all kinds from the fertile
province of Fayoum, stores for the roads; and at Port Said and
Suez material from the outside world was trans-shipped on
to them for conveyance to Kantara. Loaded almost down to
the water's edge they came to the jetties, tied up, emptied, and
went away for more. Great wooden warehouses were built to
receive the cargoes, and almost daily the number grew until
they extended for miles down the Canal bank.

It would appear that the zenith of construction had now

52

been reached, but as it became increasingly evident that the Turks would never again reach the Canal, so it was obvious that something more ambitious must be attempted, if the great advance was to be carried out successfully. For the feluccas were limited by their size to carrying articles of small compass, capable of being unloaded by hand; the larger implements of war were beyond them.

Thus the engineers had to tackle the enormously difficult problem of widening and deepening the Canal sufficiently to allow ocean-going steamers to come close in to the bank and discharge their cargoes directly on to the shore; this would serve the double purpose of time-saving in the transport of material, and lightening the strain on the ports of Alexandria and Port Said, which had borne a heavy burden since the war began. It was no mean undertaking to make fundamental alterations in a great artery like the Suez Canal. No diminution in the traffic was permissible, since not only ourselves but the larger needs of the troops in France had to be considered. Supplies were being brought from Australia and India in large quantities, and most of the vessels had to pass through the Canal. Thus the alterations had to be carried out while, as it were, the day's work was going on, and it took months of patient toil before the end was in sight. Indeed, I am not sure that the troops were not already in Palestine before the first ocean-going steamer drew up to its berth in the newly-made docks.

What made the business more difficult still was the incredible shortage of skilled labour. Owing to our deplorable predilection in the army for putting square pegs into round holes, there were trained engineers sweeping out mess-huts or carrying stretchers; capable mechanics digging holes or grooming horses; and skilled draughtsmen addressing envelopes and writing: "Passed to you, please, for information and necessary action," on documents referring to the momentous question as to whether No. 54321 Dr. Jones, R.H.A., should have a pair of new breeches at the public expense or pay for them out of his beer-money. All were very necessary tasks, no doubt, but requiring the right men to do them; and the engineers very urgently wanted the right men, too, not merely for making the docks, but for their multifarious activities in the field. In their search for them they went through the army like a scourge.

A trade-testing centre was established at Kantara to which from every unit in the field or at the base came butchers, bakers, miners, moulders, brass-founders, electrical, mechanical, and civil engineers, draughtsmen, men accustomed to all kinds of steel and iron work, and railwaymen. All were tested practically in their respective trades by an expert in that trade, after which they were graded according to their proficiency and knowledge, transferred to the engineers, and sent about their proper business. By this system the cream of the skilled trades was obtained; and there was the double satisfaction that the men were not only working at the jobs for which they were best suited, but were helping materially to win the war.

The scheme went further. As the supply of really skilled men was necessarily somewhat small, and the need great, the apprentices and semi-qualified men were eliminated from other units by the same process of selection, sent to Kantara and given the opportunity of learning more of their trade, being tested from time to time to learn the measure of their progress, until they could take their places amongst the qualified men. Thus a constant supply was more or less assured, and the O.C. of a Field Company of Engineers requiring, say, a fitter or a wheelwright or a moulder, merely asked for them in much the same way as one orders a ton of coal; if the goods, so to speak, were to be had, he got them.

So sedulously were the records of trades kept that the authorities never lost touch of the men, especially of those engaged in intricate or delicate trades. On one occasion a skilled instrument-maker journeyed 1200 miles to Kantara in order to do a job for which he happened to be the only man at the moment available! And similar cases might be multiplied almost indefinitely.

While provision was laboriously being made to fit Kantara for its mission as a great base, means had to be prepared to send forward supplies and material to the army in the desert, now feeling its way towards Romani. One of the delights of the Egyptian campaign was that no sooner was one obstacle overcome than another rose up to bar the way. It was a useful aid to the development of character, no doubt, and at any rate a powerful incentive to the acquirement of a comprehensive vocabulary.

There was this ever-recurring question of transport. Hitherto the bulk of the carrying-work had been done by the much-abused camel, the ideal animal for the job, for he thrives where a horse will starve, and he need not be watered more than once every three days, or even less often, if necessary. His only drawback is his comparative slowness of gait. He can do his steady two and a half miles an hour for ever and ever, but if an army suddenly takes it into its head to advance twenty miles the camel must somehow go with it, and some quicker form of transport must be organised behind to supplement his work.

Thus, born of urgent need, the Railway Operating Division came into being, and set about the construction of a railway. The difficulties at the outset were enormous. Not only was the line required quickly to follow in the wake of the now steadily advancing army, but transport had to be arranged to bring material from the docks to the railway in embryo. Again the camels stepped into the breach, and daily long convoys carrying stones and sleepers and rails went forward into the desert and dropped their loads at places appointed along the proposed route.

Another and more serious trouble was the lack of men; for if the engineers had to scour the army for men to make and organise the water-transport, they had to use a fine comb to get the railwaymen, since only a small percentage had been allowed to enlist in the first place. However, by the aid of the system aforementioned, they got together sufficient to meet the needs of the moment. The bulk of the men had originally been recruited from two of the great English railways, and either by accident or design, probably the latter, the authorities kept the men from each railway in separate companies.

The keenness was terrific. Right from the moment when the railway first thrust its shining tentacles across the desert, there was a competition between the two as to which could lay the longer stretch of line in a day's work. Aided and abetted by the Camels and the E.L.C., they progressed at an astonishing pace, and in spite of all drawbacks from sand and the terrible heat, an average rate of one mile of line a day was maintained.

To the uninitiated it may seem that railway-making in the desert is a mere matter of dropping sleepers on to the sand as far as you want to go, bolting the rails on to them, and running non-stop expresses at once. On the contrary, except that no rivers had to be bridged nor tunnels made, laying a line over the desert requires at least as much care and preparation as elsewhere. For if there is one thing certain about this unchanging land, it is that the contours of the desert are eternally changing. The sand is continually silting, and a *khamseen* may alter the whole surface of the land, yet to the eye it remains substantially the same. It is only when you come to study the desert in terms of the theodolite, so to speak, that you discover its mutability; that which is a hill to-day may be a plain tomorrow.

All this had to be considered in making the railway-bed, which must have a firm foundation of stones and a suitable embankment. To put a mile of line down in a day and maintain that rate is, then, a fairly creditable feat. Each company worked alternate days; sometimes one company would beat the record by a few yards, sometimes the other; there was little to choose between them from the point of view of efficiency.

Here is a story, which I like to think is true, of their intense rivalry and its results.

As the railway was approaching Romani—this was just before the battle—one company laid down a stretch of line beating the previous best by some distance, after which they mentioned the matter casually to their rivals, and retired to rest in the fond belief that they had effectually "put it acrost 'em." Life is full of surprises, however. In the chill hour before dawn the next day a band of soldiers, breathing profanity and determination, crept across the desert to the line, and made an attack on that record. All through the day they toiled, pausing seldom for rest or refreshment, and oblivious to everything but their work. Towards sunset a triumphant shout proclaimed that victory had been won. At about the same moment from the rear came another shout, which had in it nothing of triumph, the shout of a man anxious to do some one grievous bodily hurt.

It was a heated staff-officer who had been sent by the general to know what the dickens they meant by getting in advance of the troops, whether they knew that they were pushing the railway right into the Turkish lines, and whether it was intended for our use or the Turks', etc. etc. It had apparently taken the staff most of the day to see what was going on, but the facts were none the less correct; for the railwaymen in their enthusiasm had failed to notice anything but their general direction, which was, of course, perfectly accurate; the fact that they had indeed advanced beyond our lines had utterly escaped them! Later, the general is reported to have written praising the keenness of the two companies, but recommending that in future zeal should be tempered with discretion.

Whether the story be true or not is really immaterial, because the incident could quite easily have happened with these railwaymen; it took much to stop them.

Not only here but at Kantara a like activity prevailed. A line was laid running alongside the Canal bank, so that the wharves, and later the docks, were in direct connection with the main line: thus ships and feluccas could be unloaded direct on to a train. From this line also branch lines were made running through the main supply and ordnance depots, again to preserve continuity and save time. A network of sidings was constructed, and soon covered many acres of ground; sheds were built for the locomotives; repairing plant was installed and signalling apparatus erected; handsome stone buildings sprang up as station offices; and, in short, one morning Kantara woke up to find itself the possessor of a railway terminus complete in every essential detail, even down to a buffet for the troops.

Up to the end the engineers were incessantly extending and improving Kantara. In time substantial churches were built alongside Dueidar Road; playing areas were laid out and cinemas erected for the troops; and the Y.M.C.A. built lounges, concert-halls, and tea-rooms. Of these it is not necessary to speak, for they were but the trimmings of the place.

The principal attempt has been to present Kantara as it looked to us when we crossed the bridge that moonlight night in the early spring of 1917: a cluster of feluccas with their great masts bared to the sky; long lines of neat huts fringing the Canal; behind them a vast white city; away to the north the twinkling lights of the railway station; then, when the last gun and the last wagon had rumbled over the bridge, the broad highroad leading eastward to the desert and thence into Palestine.

It seemed a very miracle to us, who had lived there little more than a year before, that so much had been done. Possibly our inquiring friends, had they been riding with us that night, through those five miles of sleeping tents, would have believed the evidence of their own eyes.

If visual testimony were insufficient, let the simple fact be recorded that we had to stop and ask the way!

Chapter 5

The Wire Road

I suppose there is on each of our many battle-fronts at least one familiar road; by which I mean a road traversed regularly of necessity by the many, and remembered afterwards with feelings either of anger, of respect, or of loathing, almost as one regards a human being.

I have heard men who fought in France speak of a certain road between Bapaume and Peronne with a metaphorical lift of the cap; a famous Irish division who came to Egypt from Salonica, utter winged words when they refer to a heart-breaking road in that malaria-stricken hole; and presumably it is the same elsewhere.

We, too, have our road—perhaps the most famous, as it is the oldest, of them all. It is famous not merely in its present aspect, but chiefly for its history, extending almost as far back into antiquity as Time itself, and for its hallowed memories; it has, moreover, seen many, many wars.

It is the great caravan route from Egypt into Palestine. Eastwards from Kantara it runs, across the desert of Northern Sinai to El Arish, thence onwards to Jerusalem and Damascus. Phoenicians, Romans, Moslems, and Jews have traded and fought over it. Napoleon came this way in his hurried dash into Egypt, and here, too, most of his army left their scattered bones. It is hallowed by the journey of Joseph and Mary with the infant Christ, fleeing into Egypt from the wrath of Herod.

59

Nineteen hundred odd years later the British soldier fought his way eastwards and northwards over the same route on his mission to free the Holy Land from the ambitions of a modern Herod. Almost the sole reason for its existence is the wells. The original road, considered as such, is singularly unimpressive; it is, in fact, little more than a mere track in the desert, when it is visible at all, for the ever-shifting sand obliterates as fast as they are made the imprints of marching feet.

The wells regulate the general direction, as on all the great caravan routes, and also the distance of a day's march. One may be quite certain that the ancients did no unnecessary wandering in the desert, but took the shortest cut from one well to another. Hence, the track follows its milestones, as it were, and not vice versa.

We did the same, and until the laying of the pipe-line rendered the army more or less independent of them, all the marching and fighting in this desert were for the possession of the wells that marked the old-time halting-places. Nowadays, the military road runs alongside the older one.

It is no ponderous affair of logs, or stones, or asphalt; a very simple, homely thing went to its making: just wire-netting, with a two-inch mesh, the kind one uses for the fowl-run! Laid in three rows, and pegged down on to the sand, it is wide enough for infantry comfortably to march four abreast. Simple though it sounds, it is astonishingly effective, and, indeed, the sensation is almost that of walking on a hard, macadamised road.

The cavalry may not use the road, nor the transport, nor the artillery; it is exclusively for the infantry, and deservedly so, for only they, who, carrying a rifle and pack, have trudged along ankle-deep over that blistering desert, know what a relief it is to march for an hour or two on a good road. And further, it is the infantry who bear the heat and burden of the day. All through the summer of 1916—and I have said elsewhere what manner of summer it was—they fought and

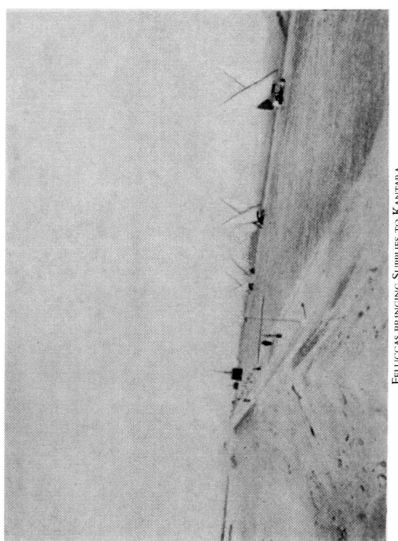

FELUCCAS BRINGING SUPPLIES TO KANTARA

died that the way might be made clear for those to follow them, and that the engineers could lay the road some of them would never use.

People at home generally are under the impression that there was no fighting in Egypt at all for two years; that the troops there had no difficulties to encounter nor hardships to endure; and that life, in fact, was one grand, sweet song.

Ask the men from Lancashire, or the Scottish Territorial division who came from the horrors of Gallipoli, or the Yeomanry, or the Australian Light Horse, what they think of the song of the Sinai desert, as they heard it in 1916!

I fear that in this matter I am somewhat like Mr. Dick with King Charles' head; yet it is maddening, and indeed most monstrously unfair, that the work of these splendid men should pass unnoticed and unsung. It need hardly be said that I am not complaining on my own behalf. Heaven forbid! At the time the wire road was being made, we were away out East of Suez, digging holes and making other roads, with merely the discomforts peculiar to the place to endure.

But to the pioneers the glory, who conquered both the desert and the Turks. There was none of the pomp and circumstance of war about their work, no great concentration of men and horses and guns, no barrage nor heavy gunfire for days in preparation for an attack, no aircraft—though the ancient buses in use did wonderful work, considering their limitations—nothing but a few thousand men in their shirt sleeves; and it was out of their sweat and blood that the way was made clear for them that followed.

Everywhere and in every respect, save courage and endurance, the enemy held the advantage. During his slow retreat the choice of ground almost invariably lay with him; and the Turk has a nice eye for position, as we found on many occasions bitterly to our cost. Nor did he miss any opportunity of making a surprise attack, as on that black Easter Sunday of 1916, when he crept up and fell upon the Yeomanry at Katia and Oghratina, two cavalry posts east of Kantara. Under cover of a desert mist the Turks crawled past the outposts and fell upon the sleeping men in overwhelming numbers.

Yet even these odds were not too great. Taken completely by surprise as they were, the Yeomanry fought with everything they could lay their hands on: sabres, rifles, bayonets, mallets, pegs, even with bare fists, asking no quarter and with no thought of surrender. They knew that no help could possibly arrive in time, for the Turks attacked simultaneously at both places; yet they fought on with desperate courage until the Turks at length retired, unable to break the gallant little band.

And who now remembers the names of these places, except the relatives of those who fell there, and the few who, fighting, came safely through? They were little affairs of outposts, mere skirmishes, perhaps, but they paved the way for the larger task. And who now speaks of Romani? Yet it was one of the decisive battles of the war. Here the Turks made a magnificently organised attempt to break through our defences and reach the Canal. It was indeed a wonderful feat to bring an army of nearly 30,000 men across a sparsely watered desert, with their nearest railhead a hundred and fifty miles away. We found it difficult enough later with the help of the railway. Not only did they bring an army, but dragged, on sledges, heavy guns up to 8 inches in calibre with them—a very rude shock to our experts, who pronounced it impossible until they saw our observation posts on the summit of Kattigannit literally plastered with heavy shells.

For nearly a fortnight the Turks struggled to get through. First they tried to break down our defences between Romani and the sea. Foiled in this they swung across to the other flank and fought for possession of the chain of hills dominating this region. Mount Royston, Mount Meredith, and the long, whale-backed Wellington Ridge all changed hands at least once, and the last-named became the principal Turkish position, around which a terrible struggle raged for nearly two days.

The infantry and dismounted cavalry advancing to the attack had first to cross a broad stretch of uneven country as bare as the back of the hand, and swept from end to end by machine-guns. They sank over the boot-tops into the sand at every step, they were hampered by their equipment, and the blazing August sun made their rifles almost too hot to hold.

Painfully the long line struggled on, halted a little while and lay down, for human endurance has its limits, then went forward again. So, alternately forcing themselves through the sand, and lying down for very want of breath, the sweating men came to the foot of the ridge, sadly decimated in numbers, but unconquerable in their determination to get to the top.

Now they made a last great effort, and, swearing, sliding, sometimes sinking up to the knees, sometimes crawling, and all the time swept by a murderous fire, these wonderful men reached the redoubt and at length got to grips, only to be thrust back again by the no less determined Turks.

Again they came, a mere handful, and again they were driven back. Now a second wave reached the slope, and with the shattered remnant of the first made a great rush, obtained a footing and kept it. It was sheer hand-to-hand fighting of the fiercest kind; every man marked his man and went for him with the bayonet.

The Turks gave back thrust for thrust; they yielded no ground, but died where they stood. Quarter was neither asked nor given. Men fought in little groups until one or the other was wiped out, when the survivors rushed away and gave a hand elsewhere. And at last victory was to the strong, and Wellington Ridge was won—at a price.

Yet although the capture of the ridge turned their position, the Turks elsewhere retired but slowly, contesting every attempt at an advance with most bitter determination.

All through these scorching days the battle raged, and even the fine work of the cavalry failed to break them, for they knew that with every yard they retreated, their cherished dream of crossing the Canal receded farther and farther. It was not a question of *reculer pour mieux sauter*, the Turks knew that if they were driven out of a position they left it for good; wherefore they fought with the courage of despair. They had to go, however, for nothing human could stand against the inexorable advance of our men.

But the fighting, bloody and desperate though it was, was not the worst of the hardships endured by both victor and vanquished; many things pass unnoticed in the heat of battle. It is afterwards, when the pursuit is spent, and a man thinks of a meal and a drink, that he counts up his hurts. In the fight he has perhaps thrown away his haversack to give himself more freedom of movement, or a chance bullet has pierced his water-bottle; and there he is, miles from anywhere, with neither rations to eat nor water wherewith to slake the thirst that seems to be gnawing his throat away. Nor has he the chance of obtaining more, except from a comrade.

There were small parties of men concerned in the remoter fighting who advanced too far, and when night fell, lost touch with the main body. For forty-eight hours some of them were lost in the desert; water and rations were soon all gone, and they suffered intolerably with the heat. Hunger they could endure, but they were driven to dreadful and unnameable expedients to quench the thirst that consumed them. When at last they did find their comrades, their tongues and lips were so blackened and swollen that the first drinks had to be given through a straw.

Imagine the plight of the wounded, lying on the slopes of Wellington Ridge and elsewhere, racked with pain, and tortured almost to madness by flies and thirst, exposed for hours to the merciless rays of the sun, until the stretcher-bearers, working though they were like men inspired, had the opportunity to carry them away to the rear.

And then, what? Here were no swift, easy-running cars, no comfortable hospital-trains to whirl them down to a Base where there were baths, clean linen, and kindly sisters to make them forget what had passed. Instead, two or three bell-tents wherein doctors and orderlies, worked almost to a standstill and rocking on their legs with fatigue, strove to dress the wounds of the maimed and shattered men.

Nor was this the worst. After the wounds had been cleansed and bound up as well as might be, came the journey down to Kantara. The lucky few were carried in sand-carts, but the large majority went on camel-back, lying in a *cacolet*. A *cacolet* is a kind of stretcher-bed with a rail round it, and a hood over the top to protect the occupant from the sun. Each camel carried two *cacolets*, one clamped to each side of a specially constructed saddle. To a wounded man the motion was the very refinement of torture, especially if the other *cacolet* were occupied by a heavier man. At one moment the *cacolet* swung high in the air, and the sufferer was banged against the lower rail; the next, it was at the other extreme, and he was almost thrown out—there was no rest from the maddening motion until a merciful unconsciousness brought relief to the tortured body.

By means of cunningly placed blankets the medical authorities did all that was humanly possible to mitigate the terrible jolting, but with all their care and ingenuity even the shortest journey in a *cacolet* was a nightmare.

The miracle was that even the uninjured men could endure so much. One could—and did—live on bully-beef and biscuits for weeks at a time and take no harm, provided one could get water. But the Turks had a habit of poisoning the wells as they retreated, and the most stringent orders had therefore to be issued, forbidding men to drink of water unexamined by a medical officer. It was pitiful to see the horses, too, after two or three days' hard riding, watered perhaps once in all that time; for the lightest driver or cavalryman, with his equipment, rides at least eleven stone, a heavy burden to carry over the sand in the heat.

Out of such troubles was the victory of Romani won. It meant that a few more miles of railway could be built; that the wire road could go forward once more; that the pipe-line could carry onward its precious freight; and that the Canal was safe. Of like nature, too, were the victories at Bir El Abd, where the Turks held on to their positions with such extraordinary tenacity that it was literally touch-and-go which side retreated; but those dour Scotchmen could take a deal of hammering, and the Turks had to go in the end; at Mazar, at Maghdaba, and at Rafa, on the border, where the Turkish dream of an Ottoman Egypt was shattered for ever. So they retreated into Palestine, with the shadow of yet a greater cataclysm upon them.

This, then, was the work accomplished by those early pioneers, and scarcely the half of it has been told. Let those who sat in their arm-chairs in England demanding querulously what we were doing in Egypt judge of their achievement.

They marched and toiled and fought—a few scattered, solitary graves mark the places where some of them lie buried. If they fought only in their thousands and not in their tens of thousands, the reason is simple: in all the peninsula between Kantara and El Arish the wells may be numbered on the fingers, and before an army can be used, its means of procuring food and drink must be assured. Water did not exist in sufficient quantities for a big army, nor was there any transport available for food. Dysentery, heat, flies, bad water, no water—they took them as a matter of course, and went forward nor stayed for any man.

In the course of twelve months they cleared the enemy out of a hundred and fifty miles of desert over which they built the railway, laid the pipe-line, and made the wire road, that their comrades who followed later might come safely and quickly to the Great Adventure over the border.

And these are their memorials, for they did a great work.

Chapter 6

The Long, Long Trail

The British soldier on the march is really rather a wonderful person; he is so entirely self-contained. This, by the way, refers not so much to his manners as to his methods.

To begin with, he has to carry all his goods and chattels on his person. The infantryman has his pack and equipment, a wonderful assortment of articles that bristle out from him like the quills on a porcupine, and which he generally describes as "The Christmas Tree"; with which, too, he can do most things, from preparing a meal for himself to digging a trench.

The "gunners" and the cavalry, while fortunately for them not obliged to carry a pack, may take only what they can cram into their haversacks or pack on to their saddles, and that is necessarily somewhat limited in quantity. Kit bags and tents are of course left behind. In fact, when we struck the caravan road leading into Palestine we were destined for many months to a nomadic, gipsy-like existence, sleeping under the stars, and scratching for our meals with what means our ingenuity could devise. I remember seeing, the morning we left Kantara, a steam-roller puffing stolidly along the road—a ludicrous sight, too, there in the desert—and it seemed when we left it behind that we were snapping the last link which bound us to civilisation. As it transpired later, this particular trek was considerably more civilised than any we had hitherto taken; we had, in fact, most of the ha'pence and few of the kicks experienced by our predecessors. Indeed, we had ample opportunity of seeing how much they had accomplished, and how extraordinarily well it had been done.

As I have said, the railway for the most part ran parallel with the road, and at no time was it more than a mile away. Every third day the train brought a load of forage and rations to the appointed stations on the line, to which each unit sent its representatives to bring back supplies for three days.

We had, if I remember rightly, fresh meat and bread for one day, and the remaining two bully-beef and biscuits; in any case we certainly did not starve. Watering was rather more difficult, particularly just now, for the Bedouins, who some-how manage to exist in this barren land, were very fond of tampering with the pipe-line and then fading quietly away, with the result that exasperated engineers were dashing up and down with white lead and repairing tools, so that wa-ter was generally unobtainable from this source. The trouble was that although the main was covered up, the continual movement of the sand left it exposed to the tender mercies of these Bedouins. Later, the engineers gathered scrub from the surrounding desert and replanted it in the embankment covering the pipe, thus binding the sand, and forming a firm and permanent barrier to future depredations. To obviate the present difficulty, large cisterns were erected at most of the stations on the line, and were fed from two-thousand gallon tanks brought up from Kantara on the train. Always our first business at the end of a day's trek was to ride away and look for the railway station, with its one solitary hut and the half-dozen tents occupied by the water-guard.

I have ventured to mention these details in order to show how very carefully the move across the desert of even one small unit, especially a mounted unit, had to be planned out from beginning to end, if it was to have rations and water in the right place at the right time; the least hitch and men had to go foodless for a day or even longer.

At Pelusium we had an exciting moment: the country hereabouts consists of a series of hillocks from behind one of which, without the slightest warning, reared up a monster of grotesque shape emitting unseemly noises. Simultaneously the horses reared up and made a spirited attempt to return to home and friends, and it was not until the turmoil had subsided a little that we realised what this uncouth beast was. It was a tank.

We had been mightily intrigued by hearing of the appearance in France of these monstrous engines of war, but as a cloud of secrecy hung over all their movements, had never up to that moment seen one. Those used on this front were much smaller than their French relations, and were as a matter of fact a comparative failure in Palestine. Whether the sand was too much for them, or the rough country over which they had to operate, I do not know, but after the third attempt on Gaza I believe they were never used. One could easily understand their striking terror into anybody, however, especially if their appearance on the scene were the least bit unexpected, for they were uncanny objects.

Another shock, but one we were able to bear with equanimity, was when we came across those desirable residences occupied (freehold) by the gentlemen of the Expeditionary Force Canteens. Even the most confirmed pessimist brightened up when we sighted one. Then there would be a searching in wallets for the very needful *feloos*, and a careful scrutiny of nosebags to see if there were any holes large enough to allow one precious tin to escape. You would see a man staggering along with a nosebag slung across his shoulder and a wild look in his eye, while his lips mumbled incessantly. "One tin OxfordanCambridge sausages; one tin chickenanhampaste; one tin pears...."

Then he would butt into some one similarly engaged, and in the exchange of pleasantries that ensued both would forget what they wanted. And the pandemonium once you did get inside the marquee! How anybody was ever served was a wonder, for the air was thick with the names of all the dainties and comestibles under the sun; but the people behind the counter were lightning calculators, jugglers, and equilibrists combined.

One of them, balanced perilously on the top of a couple of packing-cases, was hurling tins of fruit in all directions; and another performed incredible feats with an armful of bottles; while a third, standing over an immense crate, shied packets of biscuits across the counter to the clamorous throng on the other side. A weary-looking youth who had been for some time chanting dolefully: "Two packets of biscuits, please—two packets of biscuits, please...." stopped one packet with his eye. In the confusion the next man to him, on the same errand, helpfully removed the packet, placed two *piastres* on the counter, and departed swiftly to his own place, leaving the weary one ruminating, possibly, on, "Where did that one go to, 'Erbert?"

At another place, I remember, besides the packets on which were the magic names of Cadbury or Fry, the veal patties, the tins of paste, and bottles of sauce, there were large bottles of sustenance brewed by one Bass—at half a crown the bottle—and others with black, red, or white labels on them, containing a more potent but very nourishing liquid. At such times as these, it was the custom, when the day's trek was done, to "win" as much wood as possible from the nearest station—a sleeper was extremely useful—build a huge fire, and sit round it in the approved manner, singing songs and drinking wassail, which latter occasionally worked out to as much as one tot per man, if you got there early. These were special occasions, however. As a general thing we were too tired to do more than roll into the blankets very soon after the evening meal.

It was so cold at nights, too, that some nicety of judgment was necessary in order to get the best out of our blankets, of which we had two, together with a greatcoat, cardigan-waistcoat, and cap-comforter or balaclava helmet, this last a very stout bulwark against the cold blast. The first business

THE LONG, LONG TRAIL

was to dig a shallow, coffin-shaped trench large enough to contain two; it was much better for two men to bivouac together, since by putting one blanket only to sleep on, we had three with which to cover ourselves, besides our greatcoats. Nobody took any clothes off, with the exception of boots and putties. One man who did so, protesting he was unable to sleep in his clothes, found in the morning a couple of large beetles preparing to set up house in his riding-breeches, which materially and permanently altered his views.

The pillow universally used was a nosebag filled with the next day's feed, and very comfortable it was, especially now that there were no ravenous mules to break loose and poke an inquisitive muzzle under our ears. Then with our cap-comforters on, and perhaps the spare shirt wrapped round the head, we were snug for the night.

In the mornings there was little temptation to linger between the blankets, for we were usually awakened by the remarkable change in the temperature of that hour just before dawn; it was precisely as if a stream of cold air had suddenly been turned on. Besides, the horses had to be fed, our belongings had to be made into the neat roll which is strapped on the front of the saddle, the daily Maconachie had to be devoured, after which came the saddling-up ready for an early start.

For the first hour or two the journey in the fresh morning air was pleasant enough; pipes and cigarettes were lit and chaff bandied about. But the very monotony of the country soon banished any attempt at conversation, and hour after hour we jogged along in silence. With the exception of ourselves there was no living thing in sight, no sign of human habitation; even the wire road was deserted. As the nearest line of low hillocks loomed up and was passed, you knew the next would be precisely the same, and the next, as far as the remote horizon. In places the route was strewn with bones of horses and camels, while here and there a human arm or leg protruded from the sand, for the Turks did not dig very deeply, and the desert soon gives up its dead. At Romani especially the ground was littered with bones, great ravens hung over the putrefying bodies of animals, and a horrid, fetid smell pervaded the atmosphere. We were glad to get away from this Golgotha of the desert.

Another rather curious feature was the appearance in the midst of the dunes of a broad, flat expanse of sand covered with glittering white particles, damp and salty to the taste, and exactly like the bed of a shallow lake. Curious, because these *subkuts*, as they are called, were seldom found near a well, and it was difficult to see whence came the water with which obviously at some time of the year they were covered.

We welcomed them for strictly utilitarian reasons; it was a great relief to the horses to pull the guns and wagons over the firm sand for an hour or two. Sometimes, indeed, it took half a day to cross a *subkut*.

At one point we came across one of the strangest things I have ever seen in the desert. This was a small hill literally blazing with poppies! Whether some migrating birds had dropped the seeds here or whether there was some botanical reason for their appearance, I do not know, but it was a beautiful and wonderful sight; a riot of scarlet in a barren land. It was worth a bad quarter of an hour from nostalgia to get a glimpse of home, after the horror we had just left. Occasionally the dreary monotony of the days was broken by the visits of Turkish scouting aeroplanes which hovered about us for a quarter of an hour or so, until they had found out all they wanted to know, while the long line of guns and wagons broke up and scattered itself over the desert, lest the Turks should also feel inclined to drop a little present. This kindness was always denied to us, however.

Apart from these visits mile followed mile almost without incident. But there came a day, to be marked prominently as one of these days when nothing seems to go right.

We awoke to a bluster of blinding sand so that the morning was darkened with it. Breakfast in consequence was a fiasco, and very empty, very angry, we faced the trail head-on to the sandstorm. Hour after hour it continued with no sign of abatement, and with caps pulled down to shield the eyes and handkerchiefs tied over nose and mouth we struggled on. The day seemed a thousand years long; and when at last we did come to a halt, it was found that we had overshot the watering-place by some miles! Back we trailed wearily to the right place and there made the pleasing discovery that the water had to be pumped up by hand, with the aid of the cumbersome old *shadouf*. We felt then that the gods had no more to offer us.

How many hours passed I do not know, but the stars had come out and the storm had almost spent its violence, when we rode back sleepily to the camping-ground. I may add that this was the only time I was really and earnestly grateful for an army-biscuit; it was the sole article of food untouched by the sand!

A day or two later our route took us on to the sea-shore and we knew then that we were approaching the end of the journey; moreover, if further indication were necessary, every halting-place now was populous with men, all, like ourselves, marching towards El Arish, which is the only native town in the whole desert. It was here that the ancient River of Egypt once flowed until some violent upheaval of the earth's surface caused it completely to disappear. Arab tradition has it that the river now flows underground, which probably accounts for the fertility of the *wadi*, or valley, and ultimately for the existence of the town.

Approaching the place we passed a very large grove of date-palms beyond which the white roofs and walls shimmered in the setting sun. The Turks were expected to make a great stand here, not only because of its strategic position but also for its value as a port. When our aircraft reconnoitred the ground about the middle of December, they discovered that for some unknown reason the enemy had departed bag and baggage in the night, and the cavalry, after a terrible march of nearly thirty miles, had nothing to do but walk in and take possession. This was something of an anti-climax, considering the preparations the Turks had made for putting up a stern fight.

But as usual they retired with a sting in their tails. At Maghdaba, some twenty miles down the *wadi*, they left a garrison in immensely strong positions, with orders, apparently, to delay our advance at all costs.

Our horses and men were deadly tired after their long march, and the watering problem was acute. There was literally no water between El Arish and Maghdaba, and the wells at the latter place were in the hands of the Turks. However, the Imperial Camel Corps, the Anzacs, and the Royal Horse Artillery, entirely oblivious to everything but their objective, captured the whole series of redoubts and the survivors of the garrison, who fought on till they were completely surrounded.

El Arish was chiefly remembered by us because we were able to take all our clothes off for the first time in ten days, and indulge in the unwonted luxury of sea-bathing. Throughout all our subsequent wanderings in Palestine no joy ever approached that of a complete bath; indeed, it is ludicrous to note the number of places about which everything was obliterated from the memory save the fact that one had a bath there.

From El Arish onwards the track was now thick with marching men, and at Sheikh Zowaid, another spot of green in the desert, we came to a great camp, where it was easy to read the signs of a coming "show." The bivouac areas were crowded with troops of all arms, and as fast as one brigade left another marched in to take its place.

There is a subtle difference between a concentration camp near the front line and one down at a base; something more purposeful, perhaps, in the former than in the latter. There is, withal, considerable less ceremony. Here there were canteens—observe the plural—of surpassing magnificence. In the mere attempt to get near them we experienced something of what our people were going through at home. The queues were prodigious! As two canteens were rather close together we had carefully to note which queue we were in lest we should inadvertently find ourselves at the end of one when we ought to have been at the head of the other, or vice versa. In the latter case the unobservant one would have his correct and ultimate destination described with a wealth of epithet and in a variety of dialects.

The ever-enterprising Y.M.C.A. had a marquee, too, where we could sit in comparative comfort, where we met men from other units with whom we exchanged views on how the campaign should be run, on the appalling iniquity of those A.S.C. people at the base, who lived on the fat of the land while the fighting men starved—a slight but very popular exaggeration with the troops—on the possibility of a mail within the next year or two, and on similar great matters. After this we gave each other cap-badges or buttons as a sign of mutual goodwill and returned to our palatial burrows in the sand, a perilous journey in the dark across an area literally honeycombed with similar burrows, into which we fell with monotonous regularity. Our progress was punctuated by a series of muffled but pungent remarks from people whose faces we had stepped on, or who had been suddenly interrupted in a snore of powerful dimensions by the violent impact of a hard head against the diaphragm. By the time we had reached our own place the remarks had swelled to a chorus with a deplorable motif.

Next day we started for Rafa, the last stage of the march, which brought us to the southern border of Palestine. And, let me record the fact with due solemnity, we celebrated our arrival by cleaning harness!

CHAPTER 7

On the Fringe of the Holy Land

After the decisive victory of the 9th January, Rafa had been formed into an advanced base for the next attack on the Turks, who had retreated some twenty miles to immensely strong positions, of which Gaza formed the right and Beersheba the left flank, with Sheria in the centre. During the whole of February, troops of all arms had been steadily marching eastwards across the desert. By the middle of March Rafa presented an inspiring spectacle.

Every day brigade after brigade of cavalry, artillery, and infantry poured in, dusty, thirsty, and leg-weary, but in high spirits at leaving the desert behind at last. One infantry division in particular—the 52nd Lowland—had good reason to be thankful, for, coming straight from Gallipoli to Egypt, they marched and fought every yard of the way across Sinai.

The mounted division certainly did the same, but it takes an infantryman thoroughly to appreciate the joys of tramping in full marching order over the sand. The 52nd, moreover, did most of their marching before the wire road was laid. Where all did so well, it is rather invidious to single out any one division, but I do not think any one will object to throwing a few bouquets at the Scotsmen, except possibly the Turks, who heartily disliked them, especially behind a bayonet.

By now the railway had caught us up again, and almost daily long supply trains come in from Kantara with loads of rations and forage. Also the Egyptian Labour Corps arrived in hundreds and once more made the day hideous with their mournful dirge. But if this eternal chant made one yearn to throw something large and heavy at the performers, their work compelled profound admiration. They must have beaten all previous records in laying the line from Sheikh Zowaid to Rafa and were preparing to carry it forward at the same pace. It was a characteristic of the railway now and later, to appear in all sorts of unlikely places, and it was quite a common experience to be awakened two or three days after our arrival in some remote spot, by the shrill whistle of a locomotive.

The most striking thing at Rafa, however, was the organisation of the water-supply. The great tanks that had done duty farther down the line were brought up and long rows of them stood by the side of the railway. There were *fanatis* literally by the thousand, ready to be filled and carried forward when the time came. This apparently liberal provision was very necessary, for except at Khan Yunus, six miles away to the northeast, Rafa represented the only place for twenty miles whence to obtain water.

Though we could see the Promised Land, we were not there yet, nor did we know much about the state of the wells after the Turks had finished with them. Until we had advanced into and consolidated the country near to Gaza, therefore, we had to carry every drop of water with us, sufficient, moreover, to last for several days.

What the infantry would have done without the camels, one shudders to contemplate, for they were practically the only means of water-transport. Right into the firing line they would come at sundown, drop their *fanatis* and fade away again. Nobody bothered to find out whence the camels came or whither they went, but they were always there when wanted. It is no exaggeration to say that the desert and subsequent campaigns would have been impossible without the camels, both in their carrying and fighting capacity. The mounted units for the most part used water-carts, though these in turn were filled from *fanatis* brought up as far as possible by camels.

By the time headquarters arrived at Rafa on the 20th, preparations had about reached their zenith, and on the 23rd we moved out, with six days' marching rations for men and horses loaded on to the limbers, which looked uncommonly like business. Our destination we did not of course know, and we were content at the moment to be crossing the border into the Holy Land. Before us lay the gently undulating plain, in the midst of which nestled the smiling village of Khan Yunus, a beautiful sight, and one never to be forgotten. Everywhere was green; fields of young barley rippled in the light breeze, palms and almond trees nodded to the morning, and between the rows of cactus and prickly pear ran the slim grey ribbon of the caravan road winding away to the north.

Peeping out from amongst the trees were the flat-topped roofs of the village, at the entrance to which in the most commanding position stood the ruins of an old castle. Only the grey weather-beaten walls remained, but the odour of antiquity was on the place, for it was built by Saladin, Prince of Saracen fighters and conqueror of our own Richard the Lion-hearted. How appropriate and impressive a place for the beginning of the great Crusade!

Many places of historical and biblical interest did we see in our wanderings, but I think the memory of our first real glimpse of the Land of Goshen will ever remain the most vivid. Disillusionment came later, as it does everywhere in the East, yet on that spring morning Khan Yunus, shining like an emerald, came as balm to eyes weary with the aching barrenness of the desert.

The Turks had originally intended to hold the place, probably on account of its valuable water-supply, but thought better of it and retired to Gaza. When we rode through the village the engineers were already busy repairing the walls of the deep well in the market-place, one that had probably done duty for hundreds of years, to judge from the state of the steps leading up to it; they were in some places worn almost flat. The water was ice-cold and wonderfully refreshing after the lukewarm, chlorinated stuff which had corroded our insides for so long.

It was easy to see that an enemy of unpleasant habits had recently been in the place. Few inhabitants were abroad, with the exception of the crowd of dirty, ragged children watching the engineers at their work, but nothing short of a bomb would upset the average Arab urchin.

It was the custom of the Turks here and elsewhere in Palestine to allow the unfortunate *fellaheen* to grow and garner their harvest of barley or millet without let or hindrance, after which they commandeered the major portion and gave in payment—a promise! Most of the inhabitants are still waiting for the redemption of that promise.

When they found that the British were prepared to pay in cash for what they took, they acted on the sound principle that what is lost on the swings may be gained on the roundabouts. Until a fixed and reasonable tariff was adopted, we performed the function of roundabouts with great spirit and dash, though at considerable cost. Meanwhile the *fellaheen* refilled their pockets or wherever they keep their money, and lived in fatted peace.

We had scarcely halted to await orders on the outskirts of Khan Yunus before an aged Arab, rather the worse for wear, arrived with a basket of large and luscious oranges for sale. Ye gods, oranges! And we had seen no fresh fruit for months! The old gentleman was fairly mobbed, and we cleared his stock for him in a very few seconds. When he had recovered he went away to spread the glad news abroad that a large body of madmen had arrived thirsting for oranges, and, moreover, eager to pay for them.

Presently the ladies of the village came out *en masse*, all with baskets of oranges, some as big as the two fists. We had a glut of them. Personally I ate ten—this is not claimed as a record—and never enjoyed fruit so much in my life; it was a very satisfying experience.

Later in the day we rode into the village again to water the horses and fill the water-carts. As the well was not yet in full working order the engineers had dug a large shallow hole in the ground, lined with a tarpaulin, and not unlike a swimming bath in appearance. This was filled with water from *fanatis* brought up by the camels, and connected up by hand-pumps to the canvas troughs erected alongside, by which ingenious means we were enabled to water the horses in comparative comfort. For this blessing we were truly grateful after our recent experiences in the desert.

Coming back we met some wretched half-starved Bedouins fleeing into the village for safety. One mournful little cavalcade struck the eye arrestingly as it passed. At the head of the party and mounted on a white donkey rode the handsomest Arab I ever saw in Palestine, with clean-cut features and large, sorrowful eyes. Behind him, also on donkeys, rode his womenfolk, heavily veiled, and his retainers in *burnous* and flowing robes. Hereabouts the road was strewn with leaves and branches blown from the trees, and the whole made a picture startlingly suggestive of that representing Christ's entry into Jerusalem.

It must be remembered, lest this scene be set down as a figment of the imagination, that the people of this land are still the people of the Bible: their dress, their habits, their methods of travelling are precisely as they were two thousand years ago. The husbandman still uses the cumbersome wooden plough of the Old Testament, the women still go with their *chatties* down to the well at sunset, to draw water and gossip with their neighbours, as did Rachel before them, and any day can be seen, tending their flocks, shepherds the exact prototype of those who followed the Wise Men of the East to the cradle of the world.

I am not going to suggest that this incident of the fugitive sheikh was instantly linked up with the sacred picture, the process was gradual. There was first a sense of being on familiar ground, of having witnessed the whole scene before somewhere, which was followed by the transition to the Bible stories of childhood's days. Then came the inevitable dénouement, and the picture was complete. Similar scenes constantly recurred the farther we advanced into Palestine, and it was impossible that they should leave no impression.

We found our orders waiting for us when we arrived back at our halting place and at once hooked in and started again, only to be held up a little way out by the congestion of troops who had marched into the village during the morning. The cactus-hedges bordering the lanes afforded admirable protection from observation by enemy aircraft, some of which were hovering in the neighbourhood.

Dispatch-riders on motor-cycles threaded their way to the front in and out amongst the horses with amazing skill, the cavalry swung forward en route for the open country, staff officers galloped along the lanes, and in a few short moments the whole atmosphere had changed from pastoral peace to the tense excitement of military activity. Every few moments an enemy plane came over to have a look at Khan Yunus, though it is doubtful whether they saw very much, for an army could easily have hidden itself between the hedgerows of the village.

So great was the bustle that most of us fully expected that the first battle in the Holy Land was about to begin. It was by now high noon and insufferably hot, and the soft alluvial dust churned up by motor bicycles and galloping hoofs rose in suffocating clouds. We were penned in by the high cactus-hedges and not a breath of air could reach us to dissipate the choking dust. We had, it would appear, escaped the sand only to encounter a worse enemy, and to add to our discomfort, we were still wearing the serge tunics of the winter

85

months. Nor could we ease ourselves by taking them off, for this was a lengthy business, first necessitating the removal of water-bottles, haversacks, bandoliers, and revolver-belts; and orders to move might arrive while we were in medias res. The early morning rhapsodies about Palestine were, like ourselves, rapidly melting away under the influence of these trials to the flesh, and as the blazing hours wore on with no change in the situation, we began strongly to feel that the country was vastly overrated.

All through the afternoon generals, colonels, and minor constellations charged past and disappeared, and with every fresh layer of dust on our already begrimed faces, we thought that the moment had surely come to move out of that atrocious lane. But for the entire absence of gunfire, you would have thought that a frightful battle was going on somewhere beyond our narrow prison. Not until sundown did we at last receive orders to go forward till we were clear of the village—and camp for the night!

For most of us whose imaginations had been fired by the scenes we had witnessed, this order came as a bitter disappointment. Later in the evening we learnt what has already been told earlier in this chapter: that we had still some fourteen miles of the country to cover before we could get in touch with the Turks. While we had been waiting in the lane the cavalry had made a reconnaissance in some strength, in order to see if any Turkish patrols were in the neighbourhood. Apparently the "All clear" had been reported, hence our peaceful return with the instructions to be ready to start on the longer journey at a moment's notice.

The horses, at any rate, were satisfied to stay the night at Khan Yunus, for they were mad with delight at finding themselves amongst the green again. They broke loose and charged into the fields of young barley, they trampled on it, they lay down and rolled in it. Finally they ate it and had to be treated for pains in their insides. The men who were doing picket-duty in a mounted unit during the first few weeks we were in Palestine aged perceptibly with the responsibility of preventing the horses from stuffing themselves with the unaccustomed green food. It was quite enough to keep our horses fit in the ordinary way without having colic to add to our joys.

CHAPTER 8

The First Battle of Gaza

Early next morning we started for Deir el Belah, which was to be our jumping-off place for the attack on Gaza, whither the Turks had now retreated. It was a beautiful trek. If there were not "roses, roses, all the way," the green fields and the almond blossom made very acceptable substitutes. But for the cactus and prickly pear which lined the lanes we might have been riding leisurely over an English countryside. We saw as many trees during this nine or ten miles' ride as during the whole of our time in Egypt. There were few palms. The sycamore, which grows to greater perfection in Palestine than I have seen elsewhere, was in the majority and cast a beneficent shade on us. There were limes, too, and a tree which looked something like a laburnum, together with the almond tree now covered with its delicately-tinted bloom.

The utter tranquillity of the place made one wonder if the grim business upon which we were engaged was indeed real, for here there was none of the dust and bustle of the previous day. The clear freshness of the morning made us feel glad to be alive, and there was, moreover, no disillusionment in the shape of dirty mud houses, nor anything to spoil our enjoyment. It was just Nature at her very best, and in her spring dress she is very pleasant indeed in Palestine.

As I have said, it was probably by contrast with the desert that this lovely country appealed so strongly to us. Even the morning pipe had a different flavour. For a few brief hours we could forget that our ultimate mission was to kill as many Turks as possible and could plod along on our horses as though all Time were our own, wanting nothing to our infinite content. An agreeable aroma hangs over the memory of that day though it was absolutely uneventful in itself. We arrived at our destination in a state of peace with all the world, which is a most inappropriate condition to be in for a soldier—even amateurs like ourselves. However, it was only temporary. At Belah we learnt something of the order of battle in so far as it affected ourselves. While the infantry were making a frontal attack on the positions defending Gaza, we—that is, the mounted divisions—were to strike out east and north with the double object of holding up Turkish reinforcements from Beersheba and Hereira (S.E. of Gaza), Huj (E. of Gaza), and cutting off the retreat of the main body should the town be taken. What to do should the attack fail we were not informed. Presumably we were to trust to what Mr. Kipling aptly calls "the standing-luck of the British Army" to pull us through.

Be that as it may, there was—to anticipate a little—something badly wrong with the information respecting the forces opposed to us. According to this we had to beat only the meagre remains of the division that had been so severely mauled in the recent fighting on the desert, together with a few thousand infantry and cavalry from the places mentioned above. The impression most of us received was that the whole affair would be a "cake-walk." We were to take Gaza *en passant*, as it were, and reach Jerusalem by Whitsuntide.

THE BEST LAID SCHEMES....

We started at 3 a.m. the next day, March 26th, while it was yet dark, and steering east for some four or five miles came to a narrow, steep-sided riverbed. This was the soon-to-be famous Wadi Ghuzzee. By some extraordinary oversight, the Turks had neglected either to fortify the *wadi* or even to leave outposts there; at any rate the crossing was accomplished with difficulty but without interference. Arrived on the other side we halted to wait for the sunrise to dissipate the fog through which we had so far travelled. So far from lifting, as the dawn approached it grew denser, until it was impossible to discern any object more than a few yards away.

It was eerie waiting in the clammy atmosphere with the feeling that we were shut off from the rest of the world by the thick wall of fog. Memories of Katia and Oghratina sprang unbidden to the mind, and a repetition of those disastrous affairs seemed not unlikely. We felt with relief the sudden cold that precedes the dawn, and in a little while it grew lighter. Presently the sun appeared dimly over the Eastern horizon and we waited hopefully for the fog to lift. We waited....

At seven o'clock we unhooked the horses from the guns and ammunition-wagons and let them graze on the herbage.

No sound of battle came to our ears; indeed, so profound was the silence that enveloped us, we might have been in a tomb. Then, perhaps half an hour later, the fog suddenly lifted like the drop-scene in a theatre, and we found ourselves in the middle of a wide undulating plain stretching to the remote horizon. Then we saw that the stage was set and the actors were ready. On our left, their approach unnoticed by us in the fog, our infantry were marching in fours; from away to the south-west, as far as the eye could see, came three mighty columns of marching men, sunburnt, silent, inexorable.

They looked immensely efficient, these veterans of Gallipoli, tramping steadily along in their shirt sleeves—best of all fighting kit—and there were two divisions of them. Alongside them came another long column of ambulance-carts drawn by mules, beyond which, again, marched the auxiliary branch of the medical service, the camels, soft-footed and supercilious, with the white hoods of the *cacolets* swaying unevenly as they marched. Then came the light armoured-car batteries and in the centre the horse-artillery.

Out on the flank the plain was black with the horses of the mounted divisions, disposed in brigades, and on the right the Imperial Camel Corps had a roving commission. So the army marched steadily forward to the assault, a wonderful spectacle. There was this to be said for the fighting in Palestine: you fought in the open most of the time; with certain limitations you could see your enemy and he could see you. The personal element, therefore, played a more important part than when there was an overwhelming concentration of artillery on one side or the other, and as a rule battles were won because the victors were both collectively and individually the better men.

Soon the infantry diverged to the left, and the columns, moving toward the sea, were presently lost to view beyond the low western hills. We continued our flanking movement eastward, with cavalry screens thrown forward and the remainder advancing in beautiful order over the undulating plain. Within a couple of hours or so we had reached our appointed place, whereupon some of the cavalry galloped forward to keep in touch with the other mounted division operating toward the north, the armoured cars disappeared swiftly on their lawful occasions, and the Imperial Camel Corps went off to attend to the needs of such Turkish reinforcements as were to be found. We had not long to wait before an enemy aeroplane arrived and, locating us at once, dropped a smoke bomb. Hardly had the little puff dispersed when the first shell arrived with a hideous, screaming whine, and exploded with a shattering roar on the hillside some hundred and fifty yards in our rear. It was followed instantly by another which burst a similar distance in front—a perfect bracket, and we were in the middle of it. It looked any reasonable odds that the third shell would arrive in the middle of us, for we offered a splendid target: thousands of horses and men in a shallow saucer-shaped depression the range of which the enemy evidently had to a yard.

Even the most confirmed optimist could scarcely help feeling that in a few seconds we were likely to be put out of action—polite euphemism!—before striking a blow. But the God of battles was with us, for the third shell, to our utter astonishment, not unmingled with relief, never came! The reason was soon apparent: a battery of horse-artillery was seen galloping madly over the stretch of level plain a mile or so in our rear, in the direction of the Turkish big guns. With beautiful precision they swung into action and in a few seconds were firing round after round in a determined effort to put their larger adversary hors de combat. Whether the Turkish gun-positions were known beforehand and this effort part of a pre-arranged plan I do not know. As we saw it, it looked like a spontaneous and magnificent act of self-sacrifice.

It was David and Goliath over again, but unfortunately the luck on this occasion was with the latter. He plastered the battery with his heavy shells; one of them, bursting near the battery-staff, put almost the entire party out of action from the concussion alone. There was not a scrap of cover either for horses or guns, and soon the gallant gunners were forced to withdraw. They had, however, succeeded in their object—if it were indeed to create a diversion in our favour—and had in addition completely destroyed the crew of one enemy gun. With the exception of a parting round which burst near the field-ambulance on our left we had no further trouble in this direction. Subsequently we went forward without let or hindrance, except from enemy aircraft, whose bombs disturbed quite a quantity of earth.

Meanwhile on our left the infantry were heavily engaged. Their lot was not an enviable one. The natural defences of Gaza are immensely strong, and these were in addition strengthened by every conceivable human device. The town stands in the midst of a chain of sandy ridges, inside which is a smaller ring, with a wide stretch of open country absolutely devoid of cover between the two. The extreme niceness of the position lay in the fact that any one ridge was well within range of most if not all of the remainder. Without much difficulty, the infantry captured two of these outer ridges—Mansura and Shalouf—and immediately prepared for the attack on the central positions. The chief of these was the place to which Samson carried the gates of Gaza: Ali Muntar—how familiar we were destined to be with that name!—a great, bleak rock, whose terraced slopes rose far above the rest and commanded a wide field of fire over the plains of Gaza. It was defended in its several tiers by machine-guns cunningly placed, concealed rifle pits, trenches protected by rows of cactus and prickly pear, the broad leaves of which are almost impervious to rifle-bullets and even shrapnel, and heavy guns hidden in cavities in the rock itself.

It was, I think, about noon and intensely hot when the infantry began the attack. From our position on the flank it was, of course, impossible to see in detail what was going on, or much beyond the actual deployment of the troops. But the machine-gun fire, which during the morning had reached us in purring waves of sound, now increased to such awful intensity that the rattle became a roar incessant and deafening. From the moment the first waves started to advance across the open country they came under a devastating fire. They were bespattered with shrapnel from the guns, enfiladed on three sides by machine-guns whose fire swept them away in scores, rifle-pits spat death at them, and from the crowded trenches came a terrible volume of rifle-fire. It seemed impossible that any one could live to reach the slopes of Ali Muntar; yet these men from Wales and East Anglia went forward with a steadiness almost past belief, and ultimately, with ranks sadly thinned, did reach the foot of the hill. From this point they fought their way inch by inch and drove the desperately resisting Turks back through their cactus hedges and over each successive terrace until, late in the afternoon, the summit was won.

The cost was terrible: some battalions had lost three-quarters of their effectives, many had lost half, and all had suffered very heavily. True, a very large percentage of the casualties were lightly wounded in arms and legs; nevertheless, they were out of action and the battle was by no means won.

Earlier in the afternoon we on the flank had at last got on the move. Aeroplane reconnaissance showed that large bodies of Turkish infantry and cavalry were marching swiftly from Beersheba and Hereira, to the assistance of their comrades in Gaza, and we went forward to delay their advance.

A squadron of Anzacs operating from the north-east fought with such dash that they found themselves at the outskirts of Gaza itself. They charged an Austrian battery, slew the gunners and captured two of the guns. Not content with this, with characteristic impudence they swung the guns round on to the town at point-blank range! Then they sent a message to the battery of horse-artillery operating with them to ask for gunners to give them instruction in the art of gunnery, as they were not doing enough damage themselves! I cannot say whether the instructors arrived or not, but the Anzacs clung to their captured guns like leeches and continued to use them in spite of the furious counter-attacks immediately delivered by the incensed Turks. Indeed, so uplifted were the Anzacs by their recent performance that not only did they repel all attempts to regain the guns but they charged the town and got into the streets, where the bayonet fighting was of the fiercest and most desperate kind. Here they suffered very heavy casualties, for machine-guns in numbers were on the flat-topped roofs and the bullets swept the narrow streets like hail, killing friend and foe indiscriminately. In spite of this they managed to drive the Turks out of a portion of the town, and from this they refused to be dislodged, though the greater part of the men were wounded, some of them severely.

Farther east, meanwhile, another party of Australians were supplying a little comic relief. Their function originally had been to prevent the escape of any Turks should the town be captured, but as the refugees failed to appear, for obvious reasons, the Australians rode forth to inquire into the matter. A mist of obscurity hangs over their doings until the moment when they saw before them an open landau—or gharry, as it is termed in Egypt—with an escort bearing all the trappings of high officialdom, proceeding at a gentle trot some distance away over the plain. This seemed to be fair game, so with a wild "Coo-ee" the Light Horse charged down upon the totally unsuspecting party. The driver of the gharry lost his head and his seat simultaneously, the vehicle overturned and pinned the unfortunate occupant underneath, and the escort surrendered hurriedly several times over. This last was perhaps as well, for the attackers were so weak with laughter at the sight of a very dignified Turkish general in full regalia crawling from under the gharry that they were in no condition to put up a serious fight. It transpired later that the general so ignominiously and comically made prisoner was a divisional commander who, with all his staff, was apparently proceeding to his advanced headquarters with no thought of danger. It was humiliating for him and his entourage but was a highly important capture for us, in that he was one of the cleverest Turkish generals.

Another brigade of the Light Horse, under General Royston—"Galloping Jack"—operating in this area, were fighting desperately hard to drive a large force of Turks from a ridge, east of Gaza, which they had unexpectedly occupied and from which they were trying to get in touch with cavalry coming from Huj. In their successful attempt to defeat this project the Light Horse had the spirited assistance of the armoured cars whose utter disregard of danger saved the situation time after time. One group of half a dozen cars ran into half a division of Turkish reinforcements and were given up as lost by the brigade. But no! Instead of surrendering tamely the inspired madmen in the cars ran amok and played a merry game of follow-my-leader up and down and round and through the ranks of the enemy, until they had fired off most of their ammunition. Whereupon they made a final burst and got away almost unscathed—they had less than half a dozen casualties—leaving some four hundred Turkish killed and wounded on the field and the remainder probably wondering, like the nigger when the meteorite hit him, "who frowed dat brick"!

As far as our part of the front was concerned it was a day out for the armoured cars and the Imperial Camel Corps. The latter were early engaged with some of those unsuspected reinforcements from Hereira and elsewhere and suffered terribly heavy casualties in beating off their attempts to get through. The Turks were overwhelmingly superior in numbers, yet a brigade was held up for half the day by one company of the Cameliers! Another company formed up like cavalry and actually charged—and took—a position, the camels taking the hurriedly vacated trenches in their stride, as a horse leaps a ditch! I should think this charge is almost unique in the annals of war.

Yet a third company fought on until only one officer and seventy men were left and few of those were without a wound of some sort. It is not too much to say that their amazing efforts saved a large number of the mounted division from destruction, or, at least, capture.

For the greater portion of the day we ourselves had performed the role of spectators. With the exception of the contretemps already mentioned not a single shot came near us; we occupied an oasis of calm in the midst of a hell of fire—and looked on. At certain intervals we walked or trotted, and once we galloped madly for half a mile, expecting at the end of it to hear the order: "Halt—action front!" It was a false alarm. We halted for two hours—till about five o'clock, when, judging from the firing, Gaza was hemmed in on all sides.

We were then in a kind of shallow *nullah* situated about half-way down a gently sloping hill. Suddenly, over the top of the hill came a "Signals" wagon at the gallop laying a line at tremendous speed. The battery was galvanized into action by a sharp order, and in a few seconds the guns were unlimbered in a position facing due east, whence the rattle of musketry came in increased volume. Another battery tore down the hill, across the valley, and swung into action behind the crest opposite. Soon they were firing salvoes as fast as they could load, while our guns were yet idle. Something seemed to have gone wrong. Anxious eyes were turned to the west, for the sun had by now nearly reached the horizon and in half an hour at most it would be too dark to fire.

How precious those three fog-spoilt hours of the early morning would have been, could we have had them now! The minutes dragged on and still no orders came. Gradually, as the sun sank, the hideous din of firing around us died down and then ceased abruptly, as if some unseen hand had descended and shut off all the guns simultaneously. We limbered up and withdrew a little way up the hill, and unhooked again for the night. I cannot hope to describe the bitter disappointment of that moment. That we had been spectators all day was bad enough, that the horses had been waterless for thirty hours and that we ourselves were hungry, thirsty, and very weary, was worse, but that the pernicious fog should have prevented us from loosing off at any rate one round was the last straw.

We found a small grain of comfort in the shape of a well at the bottom of the hill, to which, without removing their harness, we took the horses. After the usual wearisome process of dragging up the water in canvas buckets we found it to be muddy, yellow stuff, and the horses, thirsty though they were, would have none of it. Perhaps they were wiser than we knew....

From the western end of the valley, travelling at a tremendous pace, came a small cloud of dust making straight for us. It was a dispatch-rider, bringing word that the Turks were on the other side of the farther hill in great force and ordering us to clear out at once to avoid capture.

It never struck us till afterwards that the fact of the water being undrinkable saved us. Had it not been that we had spent something like half an hour dragging it from the well and trying to persuade the horses to drink, the harness would have been removed and we should have been in our blankets and fast asleep.

As it was, the Turks were in our position twenty minutes after our hurried departure.

CHAPTER 9

The Retreat

Bewildered by this sudden turn of events, we hurriedly hooked the horses in again to guns and ammunition-wagons, slung on the personal equipment recently discarded—though our water-bottles were now, alas, empty—and quickly vacated the *nullah*.

Where we were going to nobody save those in command knew; most of us were too weary to care. Our deadened senses were hardly capable of realising that the relieving Turks had somewhere broken through the cordon; we had to clear out and, in spite of what the firing had told us at sundown, we had failed to take Gaza. That much was now obvious; victorious troops do not as a rule retreat, especially at our present pace.

Hence we had no option but to keep moving as fast as we could until we were ordered to stop.

A mile or two out of the *nullah* we encountered the rest of the brigade, and gradually a troop from one unit or a squadron from another joined the column. By now it was pitch dark, but as far as one could judge we were taking a different route from that by which we had come. Our present direction was due west, and had we persisted in following it this route would have led us straight into the Turkish lines at Gaza.

The reason, which I give with some reserve, was learnt later. A German officer speaking perfect English and dressed in the uniform of a British staff-officer, rode up to the head of the column and announced that he had been sent by Headquarters as a guide. Thereupon the column followed this audacious gentleman's leadership for some miles, until a *pukka* British officer, who had providentially spent some years surveying this very country, asked his commander whether he knew that we were making a bee-line for the Turkish defences. A startled ejaculation burst from the general, who turned to the guide to ask him if he was quite sure of the way.

But he asked in vain, for the man had disappeared!

Whether this explanation be true or no, there are in connection therewith two somewhat significant points: one was that some days later a German, masquerading as a British staff-officer, was undoubtedly captured, and paid the customary penalty; the other was that after we had trekked for perhaps a couple of hours in a westerly direction, we turned sharply to the left and continued almost due south, at right angles to our previous route. We had not proceeded far this way when we came across the remainder of the mounted divisions, and fell in beside them, a heterogeneous mass. Troopers of the Light Horse were riding with gunners from the artillery; *cacolet* camels, whose native drivers had their heads shrouded in blankets, trudged beside ambulance carts; here and there a man who had lost his horse stumbled wearily along, first in one column then in another; guns and ammunition-limbers were mingled with cable-wagons; and all followed blindly man or wagon in front of them. The army slept as it marched. Men slid gradually down into the saddle, with bowed heads, until the tired horses stumbled and jerked them again into a hazy consciousness for a few yards. Then the heads drooped once more, the nerveless hands loosed the reins, and bodies swayed unevenly back and forth. Here and there a man, utterly overcome by sleep, lurched from his saddle, pitched headlong and lay where he had fallen until one more wakeful picked him up and set him on his waiting horse again or in an ambulance. Some tied themselves on gun-limbers and slept there, while their riderless horses gregariously followed the column.

A slumbering, ghostly army, moving like automata. What sounds there were seemed to come from a great distance: the soft pad-pad of the camels, the creaking of the *cacolets* swaying high and low and the moans of the tortured men in them, the uneven beat of hoofs, and mingled with every sound was the monotonous crunching of wagon-wheels on the rough ground.

It was terribly difficult work for the drivers in the engineers and artillery, for the country now was broken by great boulders, dust rose in clouds obscuring the vision, and no semblance of a road was to be found. The lead-drivers had to keep a sharp look-out lest they ran down somnolent stragglers wandering across their path, and if the column halted suddenly they had to throw off quickly to one side to avoid running into the wagon immediately in front and telescoping the whole team. This was a particularly onerous task, for the dust made it impossible to see more than a yard or two ahead. The wheel-drivers were in no better case and in addition they had the wagon-pole to look after, and the centre-drivers were betwixt the devil and the deep sea.

Besides the rough country there were deep, narrow *nullahs* to be crossed, some of them with sides as steep as the roof of a house. Then the wheel-drivers reined in till the pole-bars almost lifted the weary horses from the ground, and those in front picked a perilous way step by step over the rocky surface of the incline.

Nearing the floor of the *nullah* the drivers loosed the reins and flogged their horses into some semblance of a gallop in order to gain enough impetus to carry them up the ascent on the other side. One of these *nullahs* was a fearsome place: half-way down the descent the path had a twist in it and at the angle of the turn was a gigantic boulder almost blocking the way. In the inky darkness it was hideously difficult to get down without overturning the vehicles. The very path itself was a mere narrow cleft in the side of the *nullah*, and the lead horses, thrown out of draught to allow those in the wheel to bring their wagon round the boulder, had to scramble up the rocky slope again until they were almost level with the wagon itself. Many encompassed the journey in safety, but soon the inevitable happened: a limber failed to clear the boulder. As the horses were making the turn the off-wheel crunched against the side, lifted, hung poised for a second, then, as the other wheel continued to move, swung farther over, and the wagon overturned with a sickening crash, dragging men and horses to the earth in inextricable confusion. The way was completely blocked, and meanwhile those behind, ignorant of what had passed, were preparing to make the descent!

A terrible debacle was prevented by the quick presence of mind of one who scrambled to the lip of the *nullah* and called a halt. How the wagon was righted and set on its way again nobody could say clearly. Men tugged at drag-ropes and strained at the wheels, it seemed for hours. But the task was at last done—horses and men were providentially unhurt. One of the drivers, who had been pinned between his two horses by the fall, had fallen asleep while waiting to be extricated, and lay peacefully oblivious to the pother around him.

When all was clear and the wagon once more sent on its way, the remainder started to come down, the dangerous turn now being lighted by a hurricane-lamp, held by an officer mounted on a boulder. By the disastrous delay, however, the column was riven into two parts and there was grave danger of one losing touch with the other. For some miles the pace of those in the rear was accelerated in the hope of catching up, but the country was so rough that real speed was impossible.

Moreover, during the long wait men had fallen into a stupor of sleep so profound that even the incessant jogging failed to rouse them. Occasionally we encountered a level stretch of ground, and the horses were urged into a trot which set the drooping figures on them bobbing in their saddles like marionettes on strings. For some seconds the absurd motion continued until the riders, becoming unbalanced, instinctively clutched the pommel of their saddles to save themselves or dug their heels into their horses' sides. Whereupon the startled animals broke into a shambling canter for a few yards till for very weariness they dropped again into a walk. So it went on for hours—walk march—trot—halt, till the gaps were closed; then: walk march—trot—halt again. Even the wheels beat out the words with damnable iteration and made of them a maddening refrain. We seemed to be marching to the ends of the earth. During a brief moment of wakefulness I found myself wondering, in a detached kind of way, if we should ever stop. It did not appear to matter much anyway, for we could only go on till we dropped, and then perhaps should be able to sleep.

At last we caught up with a long line of camels softly plodding along, which seemed to be at the rear of the leading column. Shortly afterwards we reached the Wadi Ghuzzee and attempted the crossing, which was the worst we had yet encountered by reason of its precipitous nature. Indeed, seen afterwards by daylight, it was difficult to understand how the horses managed even to keep their feet, so steep was the path.

At the foot of the farther slope, lying in the bed of the *wadi*, was an overturned ammunition-wagon by the side of which was a dead horse—a silent warning of the danger of the ascent. There was no room here for a final gallop to help the wagons up the hill; it was simply sheer, steady tugging all the way. If the strain were relaxed for a moment the wagons began to slide down the slope, and the gunners had hurriedly to scotch the wheels till the horses were ready to take hold and pull again. When the gallant brutes did eventually reach the top they were shaking in every limb as if with ague.

But the worst was now over. Some time or other we must

have reached our destination; I cannot remember. I have the vaguest recollection of placing a nosebag for a pillow, but that is all; the rest of that night is lost in deep oblivion.

It was a curious sight that presented itself next morning. Men were lying just where they had fallen. Some were stretched straight out with faces upturned to the sky; others huddled up in strange attitudes; others again lay with their heads pillowed on their saddles; and all had utter weariness stamped in every line of their bodies. Nearly all the horses were lying down, a sure indication of extreme fatigue, for as a rule they slept standing.

One by one the men stirred, stretched, and looked dazedly about them. Presently, when consciousness returned, we began to remember that it was twenty-four hours since we had eaten. Haversacks were searched for what remained of the bully-beef and biscuits, which were very hard to get down without water, and of that we had none.

In this respect the horses were in worse plight than we. It was forty hours since they had been watered. In no country, save Mesopotamia, did the exigencies of the campaign lie so heavily upon our four-legged comrades as in Egypt and Palestine. But for the fact that all animals in the army are better treated and looked after than any in the world, it would have fared very hardly with them. You should have seen some of the captured Turkish horses! It made us heartsick to look at them, so emaciated were they from ill-usage and neglect. The Eastern has no idea of kindness to animals; it was a common practice for them to ride horses with open sores as big as the hand on the withers and elsewhere, day in and day out, with no thought of giving the tortured creatures treatment for their ills.

It is a poor day for the British soldier when he cannot find some little dainty for his horse, or "win" an extra handful of grain when the quartermaster-sergeant is looking the other way; his first thought is always for his horse.

When we had snatched a hurried meal we set out to look for water. The only known wells were at Deir el Belah, whither we proceeded. We had apparently crossed the *wadi* some distance to the east, for we went seven miles or thereabouts before we reached the wells, which were, however, only for the use of the men. The horses were watered at a large lagoon, bordered with tall reeds, considerably nearer the sea, which lagoon I shall remember. There were no troughs, and we had to ride the horses some yards into the water to clear the reeds before they could drink. The bed was covered to the depth of nearly a yard with black sticky mud, and my horse, plunging forward to get at the water, stepped into a steep hole where the mud was of Stygian blackness and incomparable stickiness, and we investigated these qualities together. As I was leading another horse as well, my position was exceedingly uncomfortable, for in the confusion a trace slipped over my head and was caught by the back of my helmet, pinning me under the water. Nor were the most desperate efforts to free myself of any avail, for the horse was struggling like a mad thing to get his—or rather, her—head above the surface.

I had reached the stage where one's hectic past is supposed to pass in mournful panorama across the mental vision, when the chin-strap of my helmet broke and the trace was released, jerking my head above the surface of the water with a force that nearly dislocated my neck. The pent-up wrath—and mud—inside me came out in a yell which almost drowned the shouts of laughter from the bank, and covered with black slime from head to foot I scrambled out.

This personal reminiscence is here obtruded because the incident made the rest of the day a blank.

Orders to harness up and go out again came almost immediately the watering was finished. We went somewhere and came back again towards nightfall, but what happened in the interim I know not. At every halt I was engaged in scraping the mud off myself with a jack-knife, an indifferently successful implement for the purpose. An officer gave me half a pailful of water wherewith to wash myself, but as my entire wardrobe was at the moment modestly hiding under a thick layer of mud, his kindly act did not help very much. However, as the troops bellowed with joy every time they looked at my piebald countenance, somebody was pleased, which was all to the good.

That lagoon loomed very large on our horizon for some days. We camped near it on our return and, hoping to make up some arrears of sleep, settled down very early. The plan went awry, however. We had neighbours so anxious to make our acquaintance that they called—nay, thrust themselves upon us—at sundown. Mosquitoes! They came in clouds and very nearly caused a panic. This was a new terror. We had suffered most of the plagues of Egypt—which did not include mosquitoes; those of Palestine were beginning their operations already.

Even the tiniest creature on the earth has its function in life, we are told, but for the life of me I cannot see the use of the mosquito, which may sound uncharitable. But when, after lying down for a rest that you know is well-earned, thousands of these pernicious insects fasten on you and bite you and raise large lumps on your person, hatred, malice, and all uncharitableness are the only emotions you are capable of feeling. And these mosquitoes from the lagoon were of surpassing virulence. Presumably they had been living on a diet of lean and hungry Bedouin for many months and had found no sustenance therein; for they made of our well-nourished bodies a feast of Lucullus and gorged themselves to repletion. A doctor once told me that the female mosquito hums but does not bite, while the male bites but does not hum. That is just the kind of immoral trick a mosquito would practise. While the female is creating a diversion—and a disturbance—by her vocal camouflage, the other criminal silently puts in his deadly work. Having stuffed himself till he can hold no more he goes into a corner, well out of reach, and pretends to weep over his evil deeds. This is merely Pecksniffian; indigestion is his trouble.

Another neighbour we had was the frog—several thousands of him—and his voice was out of all proportion to his size. Just after sundown the Chief Frog made a loud noise like stones rattling in a can, apparently calling the tribe to attention. For a moment there was deep silence. Then the chorus burst forth, rose to a hideous crescendo and descended to a monotonous rattle; and this was the motif of the song. Frogs must have very powerful lungs, for these never seemed to draw breath; theirs was, as it were, a continuous performance and a most infernal din withal. We became accustomed if not reconciled to the nightly chorus during the three weeks we camped by the lagoon, and after that first night the row failed to disturb our rest, which is more than can be said of the mosquitoes. Familiarity with them breeds anything but contempt; it is generally malaria.

Although the mounted divisions had been obliged to retreat the battle was by no means over. During the night of the 26th Turkish reinforcements, now unopposed, poured into Gaza from all over the country. Next day the Turks counterattacked Ali Muntar in great strength, and though our infantry, who had suffered and were suffering great privations from want of water, put up a magnificent resistance, they were at length driven from the positions gained at such heavy cost. The Turks followed up this success by capturing a ridge farther east, from which they could shell our positions at Mansura practically with impunity, and could, moreover, prevent supplies and water from reaching the beleaguered garrison.

The daring little band of Anzacs who had penetrated into Gaza were also cut off and captured, though the Turks failed to retake their lost guns, which were proudly brought in by the remnants of the brigade. The situation now looked extremely serious, for the Turks, growing bolder, launched a most determined attack on Mansura, and in spite of numerous counter-attacks rapidly made the ridge untenable. The Cameliers again sacrificed themselves in a gallant effort to raise the siege and played sad havoc with the Turkish cavalry. Temporarily the advance was held, but as death from starvation and thirst was the only alternative to ultimate capture by the Turks, the garrison made good their escape in the second night of the battle, and the following day all our troops were on the western bank of the *wadi*. I wish it were possible to speak here of some of the countless acts of gallantry and self-sacrifice performed by our infantry during this three days' battle. Most of these, however, reached me at second-hand, and it is as well to write mainly of things seen.

The story of one may perhaps be told as being typical of many, and this story I know to be true. A man taking part in the first assault on Ali Muntar was shot through both legs, and for many hours lay exposed to the heat of the sun. Succour could not reach him and his sufferings from thirst and the pain of his wounds can faintly be imagined. His constant and semi-delirious cries for water were heard by a comrade lying, shot through the lungs, some thirty yards away. This man had still a little water left in his water-bottle, and, in spite of his own intolerable agony, dragged himself painfully across the intervening space. The exertion killed him; he died in the act of raising the bottle to the lips of his comrade.

CHAPTER 10

The Second Attempt

The business was to begin over again. We had failed; and if our defeat was as proud as victory it was none the less a defeat. Our firm belief at that time was that the fog had been solely responsible; certainly it was through no dereliction of duty that we had been unsuccessful.

Looking back, however, after the lapse of two years, it is difficult to see what other result could have been obtained even with the aid of the extra hours of daylight. We might, and probably should, have taken Gaza; that we could have held it against the undreamt-of reinforcements who poured down in their thousands from as far north as Anatolia is extremely doubtful. Further, the difficulties of maintaining a large army in this almost waterless region were enormous. The Turkish railhead was on their doorstep, as it were; ours was then twenty miles away at Rafa.

From that place all supplies and most of the drinking-water had to be brought up by any transport available—chiefly camels; this obviously could not go on for long. Opinions differ as to the wisdom of delivering the attack at all until the railway had been brought as far as Belah. The chief reason was, I believe, that the authorities were afraid that the Turks would retire without fighting right back to the Judean hills where, during the months that must necessarily have elapsed before we could attack them, they would have so fortified their naturally strong positions as to render them, if not impregnable, at least infinitely more difficult to take than those defending Gaza.

But, as an end to speculation, the hard facts were these: we had the *wadi*, the Turks still had Gaza—and intended to keep it. Inside of a fortnight, moreover, they had concentrated six divisions for that purpose. Also, they fortified an important ridge, east of Gaza, from which to prevent another attempt at encircling the town. This was a nasty blow, especially for the mounted divisions. The next attack would have to be delivered frontally, and as the Turks held all the important positions it was likely to prove expensive. Our counter-preparations were begun as soon as the infantry were firmly established on the western bank of the *wadi*. By dint of the most extraordinary exertions on the part of the engineers, assisted gamely by the coloured sportsmen in the E.L.C., railhead was brought up to Belah by the first week in April. Approximately fourteen miles of broad-gauge line were laid in well under a fortnight, which feat was a great deal more impressive than it looks on paper; for the country was now undulating and hilly, in sharp contrast to the desert.

The first cutting was being made at Khan Yunus when we passed through on the way north, and there were several more subsequently, all of which needed time and hard work. But the single line was now insufficient for the needs of the army. Another division had been brought up, and the 52nd Lowland Division, who, by way of a startling change, had not been engaged in the first battle, also arrived from Khan Yunus to swell the tide of troops. Accordingly a branch line was laid from Belah down to the seashore, where immense quantities of ammunition and stores were landed from cargo-boats coming direct from Port Said or Alexandria.

Landing the stores was a particularly difficult task. All the ships had to stand about a mile off-shore and discharge their cargoes into lighters and smaller craft. Nor was this too easy, for the currents hereabouts were exceptionally strong—several men were drowned while bathing—and the coast was rocky and dangerous; nevertheless the work was done at express speed.

At the beginning of April a notable arrival was that of the Tanks. We had left them behind at Pelusium and had not seen them since, for it was a slow business bringing them across the desert. Extraordinary precautions were taken to hide them from observation by Turkish aircraft; indeed, so effectually were they screened that even we failed to spot them.

Enemy machines now hovered over us daily, seeking information and dropping powerful reminders of their presence. In this latter respect they paid particular attention to the long trains arriving daily and also to a large shell-dump near the station, which they bombed unmercifully. A remarkable and, to my mind, deplorable feature here and elsewhere was the frequency with which a field-ambulance or hospital of some sort found itself alongside an ammunition-dump. So common was the practice that a man seeking temporary treatment would first look for the dump, and sure enough the hospital was hard by. We used to strafe the Turks for bringing up ammunition to the firing-line under cover of the Red Cross, but it seems to me that in effect we were doing much the same thing. You cannot expect the enemy to play the game according to the Geneva Convention if you yourself fail to observe the rules.

Turkish airmen used to drop messages asking us kindly to move our hospitals lest they should be hit by bombs intended for the dumps. Presumably out of pure cussedness the hospitals stayed where they were; and inevitably they were bombed. Then they moved. As a case in point: there was a large field ambulance alongside the main shell-dump at Belah upon which several bombs were dropped with disastrous results. One marquee full of sick and wounded men was completely destroyed. Several others were badly damaged, and the occupants, many of whom were desperately ill with dysentery, while helping their weaker comrades out of the debris were bespattered with bullets from the low-flying machines above. Little imagination is needed to picture what would have happened to the hospital in *toto* had a bomb hit the fringe of the dump.

Apart from this it was uncanny how the Turks spotted the places where our heavy guns were concealed ready for the coming show. In broad daylight they came over and dropped bombs with amazing precision. Under cover of darkness the guns would be moved and profane gunners laboured half the night to make them invisible—and in one case their work was so well done that twenty yards away it was impossible to see any signs of a battery. Yet the Turks found them the very next morning and made the position very hot indeed. Obviously this was not the result of direct spotting; somewhere there was a leakage; and presently it was found—and stopped.

At Belah there was a native village of sorts, a mere hotchpotch of mud-huts, whose inhabitants scratched a precarious living by tending sheep belonging to other people. Ancient and withered Bedouins—or Turks disguised as such—used to come into the camps and supply dumps and pester the troops for empty kerosene or biscuit tins, to be used ostensibly for carrying water. As these are the native receptacles all over the East they were readily handed over without question.

One morning, however, a gunner, casually looking round, observed the remarkable phenomenon of a kerosene tin perched on the top of one of several trees near which his battery was placed, and glinting in the bright sunlight. Continuing the movement he noticed another tree similarly crowned, and yet another. Some queer accident might have accounted for the presence of one tin, but three...! He reported the phenomenon to his commanding officer, who, pausing not to reason why, immediately moved his battery from what he thought was likely to be an extremely unhealthy spot. He was right; he had barely got the guns under cover elsewhere when the Turks, flying low, came over and heavily bombed the place he had just left! Of course the kerosene tins had been almost as useful as a heliograph, and who would dream of looking for such a thing at the top of tree?

Another accident led to the discovery of a much more elaborate means of sending information.

One night a trooper of the Light Horse was returning to his bivouac from a visit to a friend in another squadron. Standing by a little mound was a figure which he took to be the sentry, which gentleman he was rather anxious to avoid, the hour being somewhat late. To his astonishment the figure suddenly disappeared into thin air; the trooper rubbed his eyes and advanced cautiously towards the spot: not a trace. He was just beginning sorrowfully to think of the quantity of liquor he had consumed that evening, and to ask himself: "Do I sleep, do I dream, or is wisions about?" when he was challenged lustily from behind by the real sentry.

When he had sufficiently recovered from the shock the trooper described what he had seen to the sentry, who urged him to go to bed and he would probably be better in the morning. However, the trooper persisted in his tale, and finally the sentry promised to keep a sharp look-out on the place and to warn his relief to do the same. The next day the trooper, his conviction still unshaken, collected a few friends and together they dug round the mysterious spot. They found an underground chamber with telephone apparatus complete, which was found to be connected with the Turkish defences at Gaza! The trap-door leading down to it was hidden under sods of earth indistinguishable from the surrounding soil and the place was ingeniously ventilated by a pipe through the stump of a tree close by. The two occupants had rations enough for a siege; only they knew how long they had been installed and how much information they had gathered. The sublime effrontery of the thing! It might have gone on for ever had not one of the prisoners crawled out for a breather at the precise moment when the convivial trooper was returning to home and friends. After this episode there was a long and rigorous hunt for spies and several more were captured, most of them carrying on very innocent-looking pursuits. What made the risk of detection less for these people was the British policy, in the main a sound one, of non-interference up to a certain point with the natives of the country in which we were fighting; any old Bedouin, therefore, was a potential spy.

By the middle of April the preparations for a second attempt on Gaza were complete. This time there was no intention of confining the issue to a one- or even two-day battle. There might be another fog.... On the 16th we packed six days' rations and forage on to the limbers and moved to the outskirts of Belah, there to cover the infantry and wait till they had carried out their part of the programme, which was to capture the outer defences of Gaza. The Lowlanders and East Anglians did this in great style the next morning, and spent the rest of that and the following day consolidating the gains and preparing for the big "show" on the 19th. At dark on the 18th we moved forward and crossed the *wadi* once again: the journey this time was made comparatively easy by the fine work of the engineers during the past fortnight.

By cutting deep into the steep sides of the *wadi* they had made several really admirable roads sloping gradually down to the bed and up the other side. The way led through fields of barley now standing almost waist-high. It seemed a monstrous pity that the harvest would never be garnered, that soon it would be crushed by gun-wheels and trodden underfoot by thousands of horses. As we drew nearer the Turkish lines we proceeded with extreme caution lest we ran into their patrols, and shortly after midnight halted, noiselessly unlimbered the guns and dug them in. We had to tie the horses' heads up to prevent them from grazing on the barley around us, and muffled their bits and other steel work on the harness with bits of rag, for the least sound carries a long way in this clear atmosphere. Then, the drivers in each team taking turns to watch their horses, we lay down in the barley and slept. "Zero" was at 0530, when it was just light enough to fire, and by dawn we were up and about, tightening girths and preparing for a quick move, if necessary—in one direction or the other.

The Turkish batteries discovered us at the precise moment when we opened fire, possibly a few seconds before, for their first shells arrived and exploded in a smother of barley-stalks and dust ere we had fairly begun. They must have had some previous suspicion of our presence, for they had the range to a yard right from the opening chorus and peppered our position with extraordinary precision. Fortunately for us their guns, like our own, were light field-pieces, or casualties would have been heavy. As it was the Turkish shells destroyed most of the barley in the vicinity without doing any material damage to our guns or horses. After about an hour's steady firing, on the same lines as the strophe and anti-strophe of a Greek chorus—noise and damage about equal, that is—the excitement began in real earnest. The guns were limbered up and we advanced out of the barley fields and galloped under heavy fire across a sandy stretch to a position right in the open. We had a lively half-minute unlimbering the guns. One team advancing into line struck a patch of heavy soil which caused the pace sensibly to decrease. They were lucky, for a shell had previously burst in the exact spot where the gun was unlimbered a second or two later, which would certainly have obliterated the entire team had it not been for that providential patch of heavy ground. Another shell passed underneath an ammunition-wagon, ploughed a deep furrow in the earth and—failed to explode! There were very few "duds," however. The red flashes from the Turkish guns were distinctly visible, and every few seconds their shells exploded in a long line about ten yards in front of our position.

Our responses must have been very much to the point,

for the shelling from one quarter diminished appreciably after one particularly heavy burst of firing from our guns, and soon ceased altogether. By way of retaliation the batteries immediately in front of us redoubled their fire and spouts of earth shot into the air all round the guns. So hot did it become that once the horses were called up to bring the battery out of action; it was impossible to approach within a hundred yards, however—indeed, as soon as the teams appeared out of the *nullah* in which the wagon-line had been placed the Turks instantly turned their guns on to them and shelled them out of sight again.

But now another battery came up on our right, and the two, by accurate and steady shooting, gradually wore down the opposition; one by one the red flashes disappeared and the spouts of earth diminished in number. Finally there was a lull; the Turks had had enough for the time being.

This of course was only on a very small portion of the front, and only affected the movements of our particular brigade, who were heavily engaged on their own account. On our left the advance was making little progress. The Turks had fortified every ridge to the last degree and refused to be dislodged from even the smallest positions, fighting on till every man was killed. The Welsh Division were making towards Samson's Ridge, and being nearest the sea were compelled to move in a restricted area in which there was no cover whatever. Standing a few miles off-shore were some British monitors and a French battleship, the last-named aptly called the Requin, and these did some fine shooting throughout the day.

It was discovered that the Turks were using the big mosque in Gaza as an O.P. from which to direct their artillery fire. The navy promptly dropped a 9.2 in. shell on it—a fine shot considering the range.

Even with the aid of the battleships the Welshmen could make little progress, so heavy was the fire, and they suffered terrible losses. Not until the afternoon, when most of the

Turks were killed or wounded, did they capture the ridge. On the right the "Jocks" managed at heavy cost to seize a hill, known afterwards as Outpost Hill, and were at once enfiladed from every ridge in the vicinity and compelled to withdraw. They came again and held on in spite of their casualties, for it was hoped to reach from here their ultimate objectives.

It was a forlorn hope. All the troops, either attacking or in support, were compelled to lie in the open. They were swept by bullets from every side and plastered with shells from guns of all calibres. The Turkish action in fortifying Atawina Ridge, east of Gaza, had narrowed the front by many miles, and so well were the defences elsewhere arranged that unless Ali Muntar itself, which dominated them all, were taken it was impossible to hold on to any one ridge even if it were captured.

Farther over towards the right the East Anglian division, the "Cameliers," and a brigade of Light Horse—to the last-named of which we ourselves were attached—began just before noon to advance, after the "pipe-opener" of the early morning. The infantry had a few tanks operating with them, but these met with little success, for everything was against them. One stopped a direct hit when immediately in front of a Turkish redoubt and was soon reduced to impotence by the concentrated fire poured into it. As a matter of fact the poor remains of the tank permanently occupied this position, and until it was taken months later Tank Redoubt was ever a thorn in the side of our infantry.

By eleven o'clock in the morning we had advanced some four or five miles, after which the infantry were temporarily held up. The Camel Corps and the Light Horse made a magnificent attempt to break through between Atawina and Ali Muntar. This was the hottest period of the day; the Turks turned on every gun they could bring into action. As all their "heavies" were mounted on rails they could be swung from one end of the front to the other with the utmost ease. I cannot speak with knowledge of what happened to the Camel

Corps, but the Light Horse had a terrible time. Both units had been successful in capturing a line of trenches, which were at once shelled out of existence by the Turkish fire. The casualties here were very heavy. In support of our brigade we galloped about a mile over very broken and dangerous country and eventually came into action astride a road, with a small crest in front and a larger one in rear of our positions.

Turkish aircraft spotted us at once and dropped smoke-bombs. Again we were lucky, for the heavy shells which came over a few seconds later burst behind us on the large hill. Unfortunately another battery coming up to assist caught most of these shells and had a very bad time. One gun was dismantled by a direct hit and all its crew wounded, but the remainder fought their guns with magnificent coolness. Word came that our brigade and the Camel Corps were being beaten back by the Turks, now advancing steadily and in great force, and a third battery dashed up on our right to help repel them. For five hours the three batteries were firing as fast as the guns could be loaded. The crash of the Turkish shells bursting over our positions, the roar of the explosions as our guns were fired, and the rattle of machine-guns on our left combined to make an appalling din.

For a long time the ranges continued to decrease as the Turks pressed slowly forward, and casualties from the brigade streamed past in increasing numbers, some on stretchers, some walking, and one carried pick-a-back by a huge Australian, towards the field-ambulance away to the rear. Three enemy aeroplanes came over to make things unpleasant, but their aim was bad. One bomb dropped dangerously near the horses, who were standing the racket exceedingly well, and that did little damage. These machines did, however, harass a line of ammunition wagons, which were proceeding to a dump about a mile away, coming down low and turning on their machine-guns in the hope of killing the horses. There are few things more unpleasant than being fired at from an aeroplane: you feel so utterly impotent; and what aggravates the grievance is the fact that you cannot hit back—unless you happen to belong to a battery of "Archies." When you are a mere gravel-crusher or a driver in the artillery you have to grin and abide; and the grin is apt to deteriorate into a grimace. You can become accustomed, if not reconciled, to shell-fire; but I personally never heard the drone of an enemy plane overhead without a prickly sensation down the spine and an urgent desire for a large dug-out forty feet below ground; and there were very few of these in Palestine. At one stage in the journey to the dump a wounded Australian made a spirited, if inadequate attempt to bring down a plane by rapid rifle-fire, aiming at each of the three in turn! But this was the only effort at retaliation and is mentioned for that reason.

We had no "Archies"; and the only British aeroplane I saw on this part of the front, at any rate, was brought down in flames as we were returning from the dump. Good men gone in a hopelessly inferior machine. God forgive us, we cheered, thinking it to be a Taube.

Shortly after our return to the battery the Turkish advance began to waver. They had been sprayed by an incessant hail of shrapnel and high explosive for over three hours, and even their fatalistic courage could not stand the strain. The Light Horse were now holding their own, and soon a monotonous voice from the O.P. chanting over the wire, told that the Turks were retreating. Slowly the range increased—2400—2600—2800—until the enemy had passed out of reach of the guns; then for the first time since early morning we ceased fire.

But elsewhere on the front the situation was almost in *statu quo*. Though the Welshmen had, as stated, carried Samson's Ridge and had even advanced some miles along the coast, Ali Muntar still remained untaken. All day the Lowland Division had made the most desperate attempts to storm the position, going forward again and again with sublime disregard of their losses. But to no purpose. They were hemmed in by an inferno of fire which came from all directions: an attacking wave was swept away almost before it began its forward move.

It was horrible, useless slaughter. When it was found that no headway could be made in the centre the Lowlanders were ordered to cease their heroic attempts, which they did most unwillingly. As the order to withdraw reached a brigade which had been hammered unmercifully all day with little chance of retaliation, one of the men shook his fist at Ali Muntar and, almost choking with rage, cried out: "Damn ye! We'll hae ye yet!"

In the late afternoon the order to withdraw came to the mounted divisions and, pivoting on the centre, we swung back some five miles in order to come into line with the infantry, who themselves retired a very short distance. It was no question of a sudden, urgent retreat to avoid capture, for the Turks had had far too severe a gruelling to attempt pursuit. It was the reluctant withdrawal of stubborn, angry, and above all, superlatively brave men from positions too strong and well-organised to be taken by the means that had been adopted.

As it afterwards transpired, we had the meagre consolation of knowing that, though Gaza was still intact, we had achieved some small measure of success east and west of the town. The gains on the east were unfortunately neutralised by the deadlock in the centre; those on the west were consolidated and held.

CHAPTER 11

Tel el Jemmi and the Camels

In reporting our second attempt on Gaza the newspapers, no doubt officially inspired, gave us half a dozen lines all to ourselves. One of them described it, I think, as a "minor engagement"; from another we learnt to our surprise that we had been "in touch" with the Turks. As our casualties for the day were officially estimated to be between seven thousand and eight thousand, by far the bulk of which were from the Lowland and Welsh Divisions—who went into action possibly twenty thousand bayonets strong—one may perhaps be excused for thinking that the above descriptions err on the modest side. Secrecy is a very necessary thing in war—we learnt the bitter lesson in South Africa—but it ought not to drive bereaved mothers and sisters and sweethearts to riot and to demand the truth, as they did in Glasgow when, months later, the fateful telegrams announcing that their men had been killed or wounded in this "minor engagement" began to arrive in hundreds.

We used to wonder sometimes whether the people at home knew there was an army at all in Egypt and Palestine; an army, moreover, longing wistfully for the merest crumb from the table of appreciation, just to show that our "bit" was known and recognised. Even the rugged Scotsmen and the independent men from Australia and New Zealand liked a mead of praise, or at least encouragement, once in a while;

and when men have spent two years on end—as most of us had—in a desert land, with no one to speak to save their own comrades, nothing to look forward to beyond their daily, deadly monotonous work, they need a little encouragement, if only to save them from melancholia.

The only means of getting to civilisation, of knowing again the decencies of life, was to "go sick" as it is termed, and be sent down the line for a spell in hospital; and no one but a congenital idiot took more liberties with his constitution than his work made necessary; the climate alone was more than sufficient for any ordinary man to tackle.

But what about leave, you say? It worked out on the average to four men per battery per week—per-haps; the proviso being that no "show" was imminent, when all leave was stopped. As a "show" usually was imminent, it took about eighteen months, with luck, to work through a battery; and other units in proportion. Leave to England was all but unobtainable. Though your father died sorrowing that his son should be in distant lands, though your wife committed the supreme indiscretion, it was regretted "that owing to lack of transport this application cannot at present be considered." Urgent financial reasons—and they had to be urgent—sometimes provided the coveted ticket. There were men who, despairing of legitimate means, "wangled" leave; I did myself see an application which would have wrung scalding tears from the eyes of a stoat, whose moving theme originated entirely in the fertile brain of one of the man's comrades. The letter was sent home, copied; the copy was sent to Palestine as a genuine tale of woe. The man obtained his leave!

Sometime in 1917 a wag in the House of Commons announced unctuously to a somnolent assembly that all men with eighteen months' service, or over, in the Egyptian Expeditionary Force had been granted, or were in process of being granted, leave to England. He was an optimist; or else he looked on the Veiled Lady through smoked glasses.

Camouflaging a Tent with Desert Scrub

A Camel Convoy

The first part of this cheerful statement was ludicrous; the latter part was true, but the process was so lengthy that the war ended leaving it still incomplete! What actually happened at the time stated was that a return was demanded from the various units in the E.E.F. showing the numbers of men with eighteen months' service, or over, in the country; this with a view to granting leave. As practically the whole army sent in its name, with a pleased smile of expectation, the return suffered the fate of most returns: it sank into profound oblivion. Perhaps this optimistic gentleman, together with the majority in England, had accepted the view of the arm-chair critics, that having reached the Promised Land by easy stages we were continuing the "picnic" begun in Egypt some two years before; and on this account, therefore, we did not mind waiting an indefinite period for leave.

All this is not entirely a digression. There were times—and just after the battle of Gaza was one of those times—when the utter futility of war in general, and this one in particular, pressed heavily upon us. For the most part we worked by the day alone nor took thought for the morrow; but sometimes the desire to see well-loved faces and familiar scenes again took hold and bit deeply. If you were wise you strangled the desire at birth, for if you nursed it the result was very much more than a bad quarter of an hour. By the same token let us continue.

On the night of the battle, after withdrawing about five miles, we took up a position alongside some batteries of sixty pounders, in a saucer-shaped valley, dug the guns in and prepared to hold on till further orders. The following day the Turks counter-attacked unsuccessfully in various places, and without pressing their attacks too closely presently left us in possession of the three ridges we had captured at so great a cost.

The problem now was to maintain the troops in these positions. For obvious reasons the railway could not be brought too near the *wadi*; indeed, it was at this stage, I believe, that the branch line running eastward to our right flank was begun, and despite the constant attentions of enemy aircraft this work was carried on steadily and without pause.

Belah had now usurped the position of Rafa as railhead and the station had been greatly enlarged by the addition of numerous sidings for the reception of the heavy trains daily arriving from Kantara. The few wells in the place had been medically tested and numbered and were now in use, supplemented by those of Khan Yunus and the supply of water sent up by rail. In the *wadi* itself the engineers had been labouring incessantly since its capture to bore wells for the troops holding it. This was no light task, for with the summer drought drawing nearer every day the *wadi* was drying up rapidly. Even now, except for a few small "pockets" of water not unlike the hill tarns in the North of England, the bed was for all practical purposes dry. Eventually sufficient wells were sunk to provide a fairly ample supply of water, which not only relieved the Army Service Corps of some of its heavy burden, but released a large quantity of transport for other duties. By far the most pressing of these was to supply the mounted divisions on the right flank with food and water; and of all the amazing feats performed by the engineers and the transport service, either combined or separately, this effort was surely one of the most wonderful.

Our position was near Tel el Jemmi, one of the three high hills, each artificially built in the form of a double cross, that once marked the southern boundary of the land conquered by the early Crusaders. It was too far away from the *wadi* for us to draw our water there; nor in point of fact was there sufficient for our needs had we been conveniently near. There were at least six thousand horses to be watered daily, in addition to which their forage and the men's rations and drinking water had somehow to be brought, and quickly. About two miles from our position and under the shadow of Tel el Jemmi was a *nullah*, probably an off-shoot of the *wadi*, perhaps half a mile long by a couple of hundred yards broad.

To the eye it was as if a large slice had been cut out of the earth's crust, leaving a tapering cavity not unlike the shape of a battleship; fortunately, however, the floor was fairly flat and even. The engineers immediately seized upon the *nullah* and proceeded to transform it into a gigantic reservoir. Along one side of the *nullah* was dug a series of large shallow tanks shaped like a swimming-bath, the counterpart, in fact, of the one used for the same purpose at

Khan Yunus. These were lined with tarpaulins. Next to the tanks was a long row of canvas water-troughs, handy affairs which can be erected in a few minutes; and finally the two were connected by means of hand-pumps, each tank supplying a certain number of troughs. Other parties of engineers were busy making the *nullah* easy of access and exit, for, except in one place, the sides were too precipitous to allow one even to climb down with safety.

There were, I think, six approaches to the *nullah*, all of which had to be blasted and cut out of the sides, as sandstone was encountered after the top layer of soil had been removed; and not the least difficult part of the business was to make the inclines safe and convenient for all traffic.

All this, it should be stated, was not the leisurely work of weeks or even days; the main part of it had to be completed in twenty-four hours, to supply the thousands of thirsty horses waiting to be watered.

Meanwhile at railhead transport was rapidly arranged to carry the water, most of which had already been brought a hundred and thirty miles on the train, to the *nullah*.

Camels only were used, in such numbers that from Belah to Khan Yunus the country was like a vast patch-work quilt of greys and blacks and browns. It seemed as if all the camels in the world were assembled here; sturdy little black Algerians; white long-legged beasts from the Soudan; tough grey *belody* camels from the Delta; tall, wayward Somalis; massive, heavy-limbed Maghrabis—magnificent creatures; a sprinkling

usset-brown Indian camels; and, lest the female element
neglected, a company of flighty *nitties*, very full of their
own importance. The native drivers were of as many shades
as the camels they led, from the pale brown of the town-bred
Egyptian to the coal-black Nubian or Donglawi. Twenty-five
thousand camels carrying water! The first relays were filing
stolidly into the *nullah* in the early hours of the morning after
the battle, as though their business were the most ordinary
thing in the world!

They entered the *nullah* by one of the hastily constructed roads and "barracked" in a long row in front of the big
tanks. Then the two twelve-and-a-half-or fifteen-gallon *fanatis* carried by each camel were unloaded and their precious
contents poured into the tanks, after which the empty *fanatis*
were reloaded on to the saddles and the camels passed out of
the *nullah* by another road, and returned to Belah or Khan
Yunus for another supply. There was no confusion and hardly
any noise but the grunting and snarling of the camels as they
"barracked" and got up again, the whole process of unloading and reloading being like a piece of well-oiled machinery.
Indeed, so well was the work done that troops coming in to
water their horses scarcely noticed it.

Day and night the two long columns—the one with full,
the other with empty *fanatis*—passed in and out of the *nullah*;
and for twelve miles there was no break in the slow-moving
chain. By noon on the day following the battle two thousand
horses at a time were able to water comfortably, without congestion and without interfering with the work of the camels.
They entered the *nullah* by a different route, drank their fill
and went out again by yet another road.

Needless to say this was not carried on without moles-
tation by the Turks. It was impossible to conceal our presence in the *nullah*, since even one battery of artillery moving
along in watering order raised tremendous clouds of dust
visible many miles away, and when several such clouds ap-

proaching from different directions were seen converging on the one place, it was obvious that a splendid opportunity had arisen for a little bombing practice; one, moreover, of which the Turks took full advantage. Hardly had we left the comparative shelter of our position than the familiar hum of an enemy plane was heard, and in a few minutes a peculiar swishing sound heralded the rapid approach of some of his detestable ironmongery. Sometimes he would hover overhead and follow the long line till we were almost at the lip of the *nullah* before releasing his bombs, and this was the very refinement of torture. During the whole of the two-mile journey we sat waiting for the swish-swish of the bombs, wishing that saddles were placed on the bellies of the horses instead of on their backs. Then as we were descending into the *nullah* he would let fly in the hope of catching us in the narrow defile. The extraordinary thing was that though we must have made an excellent target, no one to the best of my recollection was ever hit. Many times bombs dropped on the very edge of the road as horses were passing, but providentially the splinters all went wide. For this immunity we had, in great measure, to thank our own aircraft, who, out-classed though they were for speed, invariably went up to harass the Turk and put him off his aim, in which gallant attempt they nearly always succeeded. Bombs dropped in the *nullah* itself had no better effect, and if the object of the Turks was to stampede the horses, it failed miserably. Frequently they would transfer their attentions to the camel convoys with even worse results; it required a great deal more than mere bombs to upset the camels, who padded steadily along, eternally chewing and supremely indifferent to the agitated people overhead.

Considering our unprotected positions and the undoubted superiority of their machines over ours, the Turks were not very enterprising. Once or twice they came over the batteries, flying low and sniping—with indifferent success—at the gunners. But that was the limit of their boldness; and when our solitary "Archie" in the valley briskly opened fire on them they turned tail and scuttled abjectly out of range.

Near the *nullah* a day or two after our arrival a few more anti-aircraft guns came up for the protection of watering parties, which function they performed most successfully, though if British airmen had been operating the Turkish machines I doubt if we should have escaped unscathed. Perhaps the hard-fighting qualities of the British troops led the Turks habitually to over-estimate the numbers and defences opposed to them, for they rarely attacked even a small post save in great force. As a defensive fighter, however, especially behind a machine-gun, the Turk has few equals, and, assisted no doubt by his fatalistic temperament, he will take the severest hammering for days without flinching.

Tel el Jemmi being by far the most considerable hill in the neighbourhood, an observation post was established on the summit from which the whole wide plain of Gaza lay open to the view. Northwards stretched fields turning brown under the hot sun, with here and there a flicker of white in a patch of dark green marking the presence of a native dwelling; westwards was Ali Muntar thrusting its sombre height through fringes of cactus; Gaza tucked away behind, almost hidden in foliage; and beyond, the shining waters of the Mediterranean. To the south numerous black patches indicated the presence of our troops and something of the activity at Belah; but most striking of all to the eye was the endless chain of camels extending to the distant horizon.

What an enormous amount of wasted effort there is during a campaign! Herculean labour to meet the need of the moment. Troops are thrust into a forward position, and to keep them provided with the necessaries of life transport is organised to the very pitch of perfection. Often the position is occupied for a few days only, when the troops are sent elsewhere and the whole business starts again.

So it happened at Tel el Jemmi. We had thought that we were merely resting there preparatory to taking part in a third attempt on Gaza. But that time was not yet. After the first two days our guns were never fired, and though a brigade went out on a reconnaissance there were no signs of renewed activity by the Turks.

On our left the infantry were now securely entrenched on the captured ridges and were obviously settling down for the summer. There appeared to be no need for the mounted divisions en masse to remain on the right flank, especially with transport strained to its utmost limits to maintain them there.

The "heavies" were the first to leave the valley, then the anti-aircraft gun rumbled away on its lorry, and finally we were left in sole possession. At dusk on the fifth day after our arrival we too departed; and the engineers were busy striking the canvas water-troughs in the *nullah* as we passed. All through the night we travelled, and the journey was a repetition of our first retreat from Gaza, except that this was a voluntary retirement. We seemed to cross the *wadi* half a dozen times and might, in fact, have done so, for it wound fortuitously across the whole of our front, and we were everlastingly climbing into or out of steep-sided places. The heavy traffic of the last few days had churned up the whole countryside into a powdery dust, which rose in such heavy clouds as to make breathing difficult, and to see even the man immediately in front was next to impossible.

In the early hours of the morning we came to Sheikh Nuran, a position which had been very strongly fortified by the Turks but evacuated without a struggle, like those previously at Rafa, when we attacked Gaza the first time.

I remember little about this camp save that the Turks had left it in an unspeakably filthy condition, causing us to spend days clearing away their refuse.

CHAPTER 12

Cave Dwellers and Scorpions

It soon became evident that we should make no more attempts on Gaza during the summer, and while both sides were preparing for the inevitable finale, a species of trench warfare began. This had little resemblance to the kind that obtained in France, where the rival trenches were frequently within a stone's throw of each other. Here, the nearest point to the Turks was on our left flank, where the trenches were perhaps eight hundred yards apart. Then the line, which for the most part was that taken by the *wadi* in its meanderings, gradually swung south-eastwards till on the right flank we were at least ten miles away from the enemy; which does not mean that profound peace reigned in this region—on the contrary. The main reason for this wide divergence was the old difficulty of maintaining mounted troops—or indeed, troops of any kind—in a waterless country. Though official-ly we had crossed the border into Palestine, we were actually a long way from the land of milk and honey; and it may here be stated that the troops saw little milk and less honey even when they did at last reach that delectable spot. In the coast-al sector—we rose to the dignity of "sectors" when trench warfare began—the infantry amused themselves by making a series of night-raids the cumulative effect of which was considerable. They were carried out on a small scale with meticulous regard for detail, as was very necessary if only

132

because the storming parties had rarely less than a thousand yards to cover before they reached their objectives.

Most of these operations were for possession of the sandstone cliffs on the Turkish side of the *wadi* and the terrain was generally the beach itself, which from Belah to beyond Gaza was rocky and dangerous and in few places more than fifty yards wide. At the mouth of the *wadi*, which had to be crossed, there were shifting sands extremely difficult to negotiate especially at high tide. After some weeks of successful nibbling, which exasperated the Turks into a vast, useless expenditure of ammunition, the infantry firmly established themselves along the coast to a point just south of Gaza, beyond which it was not expedient to go. Here they proceeded to make homes for themselves by digging holes in the face of the cliffs and lining them with sand-bags.

They became, in fact, cave-dwellers, though they certainly had army rations to eat in place of the raw bear of their troglodytic ancestors; and their caves were not dug here and there according to the indiscriminating taste of the diggers. They were cunningly conceived with a keen eye to defence as well as comfort. So elaborate was the system that it was universally known as the "Labyrinth," and no apter name could have been devised.

Long months afterwards, when "the strife was o'er, the battle done," I rode along this stretch of beach where the cliffs for upwards of a mile were honeycombed with caves of different sizes, all of them made by the hand of man. There were neat steps cut in the sandstone leading from one to the other; narrow ledges along which you crawled, clinging like a fly to the face of the cliff; and outside some of the caves was a kind of sandstone chute which presumably served the same purpose as did the banisters of irresponsible boyhood's days. I cannot imagine what else the occupants could use them for, nor when they had reached the bottom, how they climbed the steep incline again, except on hands and knees.

There were wells, too, sunk in various places about the Labyrinth and adequately protected with sand-bags. Rations were brought up by camels who made the stealthy and perilous journey across the mouth of the *wadi* nightly from Belah.

Towards the centre the distance between the trenches was too great to allow of much "nibbling" and the activity here was confined mainly to a regular daily "strafe" on the part of the artillery, and listening-patrols, who occasionally came across a party of Turks similarly engaged, whereupon silent work with the bayonet ensued, until one or other party was wiped out.

The Royal Air Force provided the *pièce de résistance* of this period of comparative stagnation. By way of retaliation for a heavy Turkish bombing raid on one of the dumps at Belah, where amongst other things a field-hospital had suffered severely, they collected about thirty machines and flew over to Gaza. Their objective was a large shell-dump, said to be nearly a mile in area, situated near the big mosque. Though the night was pitch dark and landmarks difficult to detect, the raid was a huge success. Many bombs must have hit the dump simultaneously for the roar of the explosion was appalling. The force of it shook the earth for miles round and the sky in the north-west was a vast sheet of red flame. All through the night the racket went on, as first one part of the dump and then another exploded. Seen from our position on the right flank, the blaze of light after each explosion was like the great blast-furnaces of Sheffield as you see them from the night train.

Not for days after did we understand what had actually happened; at the time it was thought to be the beginning of another attack on Gaza, and one man was profoundly convinced that the Day of Judgment had arrived. What the Turks thought about it is not known, but the raid taught them a terrible lesson; and they did not, in fact, send over another bombing expedition till long afterwards. The mounted troops were disposed in various places along our right flank, some in the *wadi*, others more or less conveniently near; and they led an existence peculiar to themselves. For our part, after resting for a short time at Sheikh Nuran, we moved eastwards to El Chauth, one of the positions gallantly captured by the Imperial Camel Corps in the first battle of Gaza. The Turkish trenches enclosed a lovely little spinney of fig-trees and almond-trees in full bloom, under which we concealed the guns and beneath whose sheltering branches we slept. Preparations for sleeping in those days were very simple: you dug a hole for the hip-bone with a jack-knife and you were ready. The army authorities had not yet adopted the Turkish idea of bivouac-sheets, two of which, buttoned together and propped up with a couple of poles, made an admirable shelter accommodating two persons. There are many worse things, however, than dropping gently to sleep in the open air with the faint scent from the almond-blossom titillating the nostrils.

El Chauth at first sight appeared to be the kind of spot where every prospect pleases and only man is vile; and as we had not had a really comprehensive wash for some considerable time and were very hairy withal, the adjective was aptly descriptive. Apart from this trifling handicap and the fact that we should have to travel fourteen miles a day for water, the place seemed an ideal one for a rest-cure. Considering that we had been incessantly on the move for the past five months the time for a "stand-easy" was about due.

We prepared everything to that desirable end. The cooks built a cunningly-contrived kitchen in a section of one of the old Turkish trenches and firmly announced their intention of cooking for us every kind of delicacy that could be made— out of army beef, onions, and potatoes!—for which pleasant piece of optimism we were duly grateful. Then we heard that an E.F. canteen had set up house about a day's trek to the south-west, whereupon a limber went forth and returned on the third day heavily laden with tins of fruit, biscuits, various meats, and something in bottles that *maketh glad the heart of man*, especially if he has a Palestine thirst. Most of us had one from Egypt in addition.

After about four days of comparative peace and quietness the blow fell—in fact, two blows. As a trooper in the Yeomanry said, when he found a frog in his boot: "There's allus summat in this dam country." He spoke a great truth. It is unsafe to trust Palestine very far, fair of aspect though she be. The first blow fell, literally, while we were having dinner one evening, when a Turkish aeroplane arrived and dropped bombs first on the horse-lines and then on us. Fortunately his aim was as bad as his taste was deplorable in coming at a time when decent folk were having a meal. Neither men nor horses were hit and we had the ironic satisfaction of sheltering from his bombs in the trenches his countrymen had made. Even that failed to keep the dinner warm, however.

The second and heavier blow was that the inhabitants of our little spinney suddenly and unmistakably made their presence felt. Just as at Belah the mosquitoes battened shamelessly upon us and the frogs burst into mighty paeans of welcome, so at El Chauth the scorpions extended the glad hand—if I may venture thus euphemistically to describe the spiked atrocity they wear lengthwise on their backs. Apparently on strike for better conditions of living they decided upon an army blanket as a desirable residence and were quite indifferent as to whether you shared their quarters or not. Often they were already in possession when blankets were unrolled for the night, and if not then, one was usually to be found in the morning nestling coyly in the folds. The moment you touched him with a stick he elevated his poisonous battering-ram, which was as long as himself, and struck and struck again in an ecstasy of rage, until sometimes he actually poisoned himself and died from his own blows!

I believe a few men died after being stung by scorpions,

certainly many were temporarily incapacitated with poisoned arms and legs. This pleasing possibility made a careful scrutiny of the blankets very necessary before you settled down to sleep; and on waking in the morning you made no unnecessary movement until you had first assured yourself that a scorpion was not within striking distance. After a time somebody made the brilliant discovery that every scorpion hates all other scorpions with a deep and abiding hatred. This provided us with a new game. Instead of killing them out of hand we caught the biggest scorpions, made a ring in the sand about a couple of feet in diameter, and matched them in single combat.

They never went outside the ring, however low was the barrier of sand, but would manoeuvre round the edge glowering at each other till one found an opening; whereupon he sprang in, tail or battering-ram first, and hammered away vigorously while his opponent tried his utmost to get round to the other's head; then he started rapid fire on his own account. Generally they ended by standing back to back and belabouring each other till one, or both, dropped dead.

Sometimes, instead of putting two scorpions in the ring, by way of variation we used to catch another sworn foe and match him against a scorpion. This was the tarantula, a great hairy spider with a leg-spread covering the palm of the hand, another of the unpleasant inhabitants of El Chauth. Against this creature, however, it was always a shade of odds that the scorpion would win, though there was a surprise occasionally. Talking of odds reminds me that nearly always at these fights some sportsman would open a little book and announce that he was prepared to lay "evens on the field." Nor was it unprofitable, for the British as a race, and particularly the British soldier, will bet on anything. One man, a sapper, made quite a good thing out of backing a scorpion which he carried about with him in a tobacco-tin. It was a great scrapper, and as it was a very undersized creature, he usually managed to obtain good odds from men who were backing larger and more powerfully developed specimens. What this sapper fed his gladiator on was a mystery; but it won many fights.

With the exception of almost daily visits from Turkish aircraft, whose aim did not improve, and a few false alarms, the days passed in uneventful monotony. Towards the end of May, however, a big raid was organised on one of the Turkish lines of communication. If you look at the map you will see, south-south-east of Beersheba, a spot called El Auja, and south of that another one called Maan. This latter is on the main line of the Hedjaz railway from Medina to Damascus and beyond, to which the Turks had clung with limpet-like tenacity in spite of their retreat in the west.

Presumably their chief reason for holding on so long was to impress the Mohammedan followers of the Cherif of Mecca. This dignitary had come in on our side on account of the revolting cruelties practised by the Turks on the inhabitants of Mecca, Medina, and other parts of his kingdom. There seems little reason to doubt that these atrocities were committed at the direct instigation of that arch-villain Enver Pasha himself. Such treatment from those who were supposed to be protectors of his religion stung the Cherif of Mecca to open revolt.

About the middle of 1916, he turned the Turks out of Mecca, killing or capturing the entire garrison, and proclaimed the independence of the Hedjaz; in which courageous action he had the support of the British Government. As his army was mainly composed of undisciplined Arabs he confined himself thereafter to guerrilla warfare and made constant attacks on the Turkish lines of communication, especially on the Hedjaz railway.

So well did the Cherif succeed that the Turks were compelled to send large numbers of their best troops in order to retain their hold on the railway. At various places on the line strong posts were established, fully equipped with the latest guns and material of all kinds. These posts were a constant menace to our right flank. One of the largest garrisons was at Maan, from which troops could easily be sent via El Auja to Beersheba if needed. Our raid, therefore, was for the purpose of blowing up a large section of the railway between Beersheba and El Auja, and it was planned and carried out with consummate skill.

The demands made on the endurance of both men and horses were tremendous. The cavalry and demolition parties operating farthest south had to cover upwards of seventy miles in order to reach their objectives, and even those operating nearest home had over forty miles to go. Moreover, it was a dash right into the midst of the enemy's country with Beersheba almost at our backs. This, together with the impossibility of concealing the movements of a large body of mounted troops for any length of time, owing to the dust, made speed an essential part of the proceedings.

We started after dark and travelled, with no more than an occasional stop for ten minutes, until about two o'clock the following afternoon. Then the cavalry struck a strong Turkish outpost and had to beat them off before the work of demolition could begin. One of our aeroplanes reconnoitred and came back with the news that a viaduct might profitably be destroyed, and a sixty-pounder battery, which had casually come up while we were waiting, started leisurely to work and laid the bridge in ruins, after which they dropped a few shells on a Turkish train farther down the line and demolished that, which concluded their part in the entertainment. Then they made tea, at which we looked with envious eyes, having tasted none for thirty-six hours, limbered up their guns, and started back as casually as they had come. It seemed to be a pleasant life in the "heavies."

As our brigade had succeeded in driving the Turkish cavalry back our guns were not needed in support, so we watered the horses at a well eighty feet deep and had to use reins and drag-ropes and anything else we could find in order to reach the surface of the water with the canvas buckets. It was as well that we had time on our hands, for the whole business took three hours. Then we had some tea. It was the only bright spot in what was for us a very uninspiring day.

Meanwhile the raiders elsewhere had successfully reached their objectives. Then the demolition parties put in some deadly work, and about eighteen miles of Turkish railway scattered itself over the surrounding country. This ended the menace of enemy reinforcements from the south, though Maan itself hung out stubbornly for a long time against the repeated onslaughts of the Arabs.

The journey back will not easily be forgotten by some of those who took part in the raid. The Australians, having completed their work, started back just before sunset. Moving more rapidly than we they were soon well ahead; but their dust lingered and most of it settled on us. Later, other parties, also ahead of us, came from other directions and added their quantum. Ultimately we must have taken the dust spurned by the whole division. It was indescribable in the *wadi*, where we arrived towards midnight. The battery was cut in two by the last brigade of cavalry to cross. One section crossed over safely, advanced a short distance and waited for the other to make the journey. This, too, was accomplished, after which the two sections tried to find each other in the clouds of dust. For nearly two hours we rode round and round each other, hardly ever out of earshot but unable to meet! This may sound incredible, but it is the plain fact. Those who have tried even to cross the road in a London fog of the old pea-soup variety will best appreciate our predicament.

In the end a driver from one section rode into a gun belonging to the other, and the situation was saved. Another driver briefly expressed our unanimous view when he said: "If this is blooming Palestine, give me two yards of Piccadilly and you can have all of it!" Finally, as it never rains but it pours, we had the cheering news that we were not returning to El Chauth, that we were to have a couple of hours' sleep, the first since starting out, after which we had a further twenty miles to go!

The last five miles of those twenty were the hardest I ever remember. The horses had not had the saddles off their backs for over two days and were almost dropping with fatigue; nor were their riders in much better state. The heat was terrific, and the greater part of the journey was over country on which scarcely a vestige of green remained; indeed, the last few miles were through heavy sand powerfully reminiscent of the desert.

We camped at last in a great grove of fig-trees near the sea.

CHAPTER 13

In the Wadi

At Fig-tree Camp we had what the army calls a "rest," which must not in any way be confused with the word that implies repose. There is nothing of a reposeful nature about an army "rest." It means that you come out of the line for periods varying from two hours to two months, usually a great deal nearer the former than the latter, and spend the time doing what the authorities term "smartening up," after the gay and festive season through which you have just passed. This generally takes the form of parades every other hour, when the officers prattle amiably of matters to which you have long been a stranger, and the Sergeant-Major takes the opportunity of preventing his vocabulary from falling into disuse. Also, if you are in the artillery, you clean your harness and polish up the steel-work thereon till it twinkles like a heliograph in the sun. Then you go out and dirty everything again.

When you come to examine the various forms of army discipline there are usually to be found sensible and logical reasons for their existence; but we amateur soldiers could never understand the necessity, on active service, for polishing and burnishing steel-work, especially in a country of strong sunlight; and there was certainly nothing in our daily duties that we loathed half so much. For ceremonial parades, of course, you turned out as "posh" as the next man, but in a parched land where you could with difficulty keep your own person clean, it seemed a grievous waste of time and energy polishing bits and chains and stirrup-irons merely for the sake of doing it. Besides, think of the hours so spent which might have been devoted to sleep! The afternoon we arrived at Figtree Camp most of us would have liked to follow the sound example of that Lord Chesterfield who, when he felt tired, used to say to his servant: "Bring me a dozen of sherry and call me the day after tomorrow!"

We rested (army pattern) for five days, and, amongst all the pother of parading and cleaning up, knew again the glorious delight of a daily dip in the sea. Then we took the trail again and in due course took up a position in another part of the *wadi*, Tel el Fara by name, the second of the great boundary-hills built by the Crusaders. Here our position was at the edge of the *wadi*, fortunately in one of the places where water was fairly abundant both for horse and man. As an off-set to this we had ten miles a day to travel for rations and forage, so the balance was about even as things were in Palestine. At dawn on the first morning of our arrival the familiar crash of bombs was our reveille, and for a month the Turks repeated the performance every morning as soon as it was light and every evening just before sunset. With enormous difficulty, for the ground here was mainly sandstone, we dug burrows for ourselves on the bank of the *wadi*. Some of them were just large enough to contain the body stretched at full length; others, more ambitiously conceived, bore an uncanny resemblance to a grave; and a few strenuous people made shelves for their belongings in the sides of their burrows.

Here we extended our acquaintance amongst the inhabitants of these regions. Scorpions we knew well, tarantulas we had nodded to, but the visitor who now invaded our narrow dwellings was the homely beetle; a monstrous fellow this, as big as a crown piece. His correct name is, I think, the scavenger-beetle, though we used a much more uncomplimentary term. He was quite harmless, but he would treat blankets as a rubbish-bin. He would seize a lump of earth or refuse much bigger than himself and push it in front of him till he came to a convenient blanket, where he dropped his load and went away for more. But his star turn was an attempt to crawl up the perpendicular side of a burrow, pushing his load in front of him. The side generally selected for this attempt was the one nearest your head as you lay; and often the first intimation you had that the performance had begun was the abrupt descent on to your face of beetle and load. Neither the fall nor the subsequent profanity discouraged him in the least; on the contrary, it spurred him to greater efforts. The next attempt would land him an inch or two higher up, when down he would come again. I used to have the most profound admiration for the legendary spider of the late King Bruce of Scotland, but after a scavenger-beetle had fallen on my face for the fifth time just when I was trying hard to go to sleep, I thought that even perseverance had its limits. So I picked up the beetle and threw him into the next burrow, and, in order that he could give his performance there, sent the piece of earth after him. Judged by his remarks, however, the occupant was no naturalist.

The outstanding feature of those days at Tel el Fara was eternal weariness; we were always tired. "Stand-to" was at half-past two in the morning, when we harnessed up and waited for orders. Often our cavalry would sight a Turkish patrol and away we went across the *wadi* into no-man's-land playing hounds to the Turkish hare. Rarely did we approach near enough to get a shot at him for he departed at the gallop at first sight of us, and in addition to his start he had the foot of us for speed. Then we trailed back, generally after dark, scratched a hurried meal and went to earth again till 2.30 a.m. the next day, when the whole business perhaps had to be done once more. The Australians thoroughly enjoyed chasing old Johnny back to his lair, and sometimes landed themselves in a tight corner through over-keenness. They always managed to scramble out again somehow, occasionally with the aid of our guns, most often without any help but their own mother wit.

The Australians were rather difficult fellows to know intimately, mainly I think, on account of their self-consciousness and an inordinate fear of ridicule. With our brigade we had been good "cobbers" since the second show at Gaza, where we were able to help them out of a nasty hole, and once their confidence was gained the Australians were very stout allies. But they were drawn more to the Scottish than to any other British troops. Perhaps it was the Scots clannishness that attracted them. They influenced enormously troops brigaded with them, as far as externals were concerned.

It was the habit of the Australians to cut off the sleeves of their grey-backs at the shoulder, thus making the shirt look like a loose kind of gymnasium vest. We copied this, and it did certainly make for comfort and freedom of movement. You would see a squadron going to water with scarcely a shirt-sleeve between them; and some of the men also dispensed with the shirt and rode mother-naked to the waist! The usual state of their saddlery would have sent a British General of the "spit and polish" type into a fit of apoplexy, for a harness-cleaning parade was a thing unheard of amongst the Australians. They used to say that the horses needed all the care; bits and stirrup-irons did not matter.

The popular idea, I believe, is that all Australians are born in the saddle and that they dash about doing wonderful things with a lariat before they are out of long clothes. This is ludicrously wide of the mark. The percentage of Australians who can ride at all is less than that in England; and very few even of the good horsemen are comfortable for some time on an ordinary English trotting-horse. Their own horses have only two gaits: the lope and the gallop.

Of course the real boundary-rider or cattleman is without equal in his own way. There was one grizzled sportsman in our brigade at Tel el Fara who could do extraordinary things with a horse, and nothing could dislodge him from the saddle. His own pony had come to him in the ordinary way from Remounts and had been a wild, half-broken creature; five months later the same horse would follow him about like a dog. The Australian never mounted in the ordinary way but would give a peculiar little chirrup; whereupon the horse at once barracked, as a camel does to be loaded, and the rider had merely to stretch his leg across the saddle and sit down. Similarly when dismounting he would chirrup and the horse again went down on his knees. Any one else trying the same trick with the horse would be received with a stare of blank indifference; and woe betide the one who tried to mount!

The highest percentage of good riders was to be found in the men from Queensland; even the men from the other states said that, though they would die rather than admit that any other good thing could possibly come from a rival state.

As fighting men there was nothing to choose between them; and the Turks hated and feared them all impartially. In this connection a good story went the rounds. The Turks holding a certain advanced section of the line sent a messenger under the white flag across no-man's-land to our trenches to ask the nationality of the troops holding them. If it was English, the messenger said, his comrades were prepared to surrender. As it chanced, a battalion of men from the Home Counties was in possession of the trenches, and the messenger returned with information to that effect. Within ten minutes the whole party of Turks were in our lines! Later, they were asked why they had been so anxious for their captors to be English; the reply was that they had been told, with much circumstantiality of detail, that the Australians were cannibals and habitually ate their prisoners; and that the Scottish and Welsh troops went one better than this, for they never took prisoners—alive! A tall story, of course, but it is reasonably certain that some such rubbishy propaganda was from time

SUMMER IN THE WADI GHUZZEE

to time circulated amongst those simple Anatolian peasants, whose sole desire was to return to the meagre farms from which they had been dragged by the heavy hand of war.

In the *wadi* the engineers were incessantly trying to improve the conditions. When the horses had been catered for, they constructed a small dam across a portion of the watering-place and made a bathing-pool where you could stand up to your middle in clear, cold water. As we were not supposed to remove even our putties except for bathing, or washing clothes, the pool was soon working overtime. On a broad, flat ledge jutting out into the *wadi* the engineers made a place where you could wash your clothes, with gutters and channels for carrying away the soapy water cut in the face of the cliff. When this was done a powerful clothes-washing offensive was begun, for few of us had more than one shirt and that, of course, was on our backs. Of our socks it could be said that the welts were good; the toes and heels had perished of overwork.

One of the few charitable things men ever said about the sun was that it dried your clothes quickly; you could take your shirt off your back, wash it, and in an hour or so put it on again, bone-dry. This was a consideration in a place where, while your shirt was drying, you wore your tunic over the bare skin and prayed that there would not be an alarm turn-out for, at any rate, an hour. When supplies are scarce you cannot afford to lose many articles of kit, nor can you call for an armistice while you wait for your shirt to dry.

Elsewhere I have mentioned, perhaps too frequently, the remarkable speed with which the railway followed the troops. On the fourth day after our arrival, it reached Tel el Fara. This was the branch line running eastwards across our flank from Khan Yunus to Shellal, on the extreme right. Just below the Crusaders' hill the sides of the *wadi* sloped gently down and it was possible to cross in comparative comfort. Here a group of engineers and E.L.C. were working in a casual, aimless sort of way, apparently building a bridge for the branch line. Turkish aircraft very soon found this party, who, indeed, seemed anxious to advertise their efforts, and bombed it incessantly with considerable success.

Every day joists and beams and stones went up in the air and every day, when the strafe was ended, the E.L.C. put them back again and added a few more. But the Turks were very persevering and literally gave the workers no rest. The bridge made little progress, but nobody worried very much. The men appeared to be content to advance three yards, as it were, and slip back two; there was no hurry over the business. Indeed, it looked like a lapse on the part of the engineers to choose such an unsheltered and unsuitable spot for a bridge; it would almost certainly be swept away by the floods of the rainy season. Curiously enough, moreover, their comrades a mile away laying the line parallel with the *wadi* were working at a snail's pace now, compared with their previous efforts, and were not making the slightest attempt to swing the line in toward the crossing. This was unpardonable, but the Turks noticed nothing out of the ordinary, and unerringly bombed the working-party in the *wadi*, quite content at finding so obvious a target. But the whole business seemed a gross waste of time and labour—unless you followed the *wadi* for about a mile farther along. This very unusual negligence on the part of the engineers was then fully explained.

At this point the *wadi* narrowed appreciably, though there was little else to the uninitiated eye to recommend it as a crossing. The engineers, however, were well satisfied, for here, out of sight of inquisitive aeroplanes, men were toiling as if for their lives; there was nothing casual or lackadaisical about this effort. While the Turks were assiduously bombing the dummy, the real bridge was being built at a great pace and without interference.

The shaped stones for the foundations were brought by the railway as far as it had then reached and transported thence by night into the *wadi*. The rough stones for the approaches and embankments came from higher up, where the Turks by their bombing activities had kindly saved the engineers the trouble of blasting. At the appointed place and time the line curved in towards the bridge, crossed it, and having reached Shellal proceeded along the *wadi* to Gamli, thence to Karm, some ten miles from Beersheba. This last stretch of line was not completed till later, for the Turks, doubtless becoming uneasy, made serious efforts to hamper the work of construction.

For three months they made repeated attacks on the Yeomanry and Australians screening the engineers but met with no success, and the line was carried on inexorably, if slowly, towards the appointed goal.

It was fairly obvious now from which direction our third attempt on Gaza was to be made: everything pointed to the eastern flank, though it should be said that the Turks right up to the last moment were in ignorance as to where the main blow would fall.

A frontal attack was out of the question. If, during the summer months, we had been stealthily and laboriously preparing for the assault the Turks had been no less active in strengthening their defences. Gaza itself was almost impregnable; and from the sea to Beersheba they had constructed a series of enormously strong works, of which those at Atawina Ridge and between Sheria and Hereira were the chief. These defences were absolutely up-to-date in every respect. They were connected by telegraph and telephone, and it could with truth be said that as far as Sheria the Turkish front was one continuous tangle of wire. Beersheba itself was in a measure isolated from the rest of the line. Indeed the only real opening in the whole chain of defences was between that place and Sheria, the Turks no doubt trusting to the exceptionally difficult country, which hereabouts was a maze of small *wadis* and *nullahs*, to prevent any attempt at a break through. Similarly they relied on the desert south-east of Beersheba to make an outflanking movement impossible in that direction. In both these beliefs they were sadly deceived, as will be seen later.

In addition to these defences the Turks were well served by their railways on both flanks and in the centre. Beersheba was in direct connection with the north, via Sheria, and Gaza, although not actually on the railway, was only about four miles from the railhead—Beit Hanun—of the other branch of the northern line. Their roads both laterally and longitudinally were in the main excellent, and they were in the midst of a country where water was plentiful and the land fertile. Finally, their immediate reserves and supplies were at such places as Hebron and Huj, both of which were within easy reach of the front.

From about the middle of June our "nibbles" at the Turkish line became more frequent and more ambitious.

The Scots made a characteristic raid on Umbrella Hill, one of the ridges south-east of Gaza, and found out all they wanted to know without firing a shot and with, I believe, only four casualties. The Turk at night-time was very susceptible to the bayonet. This raid was typical of many, and the combined result was that our line in the neighbourhood of Gaza was materially advanced and the positions taken consolidated.

At the end of June General Allenby arrived in Palestine to take over the duties of commander-in-chief. Shortly after his arrival there was a notable increase in the quantity and quality of our rations, and beer in barrels—yea, barrels—came up the line for the troops.

I am not going to suggest that the two events were in point of fact connected, but I do know that the sudden and welcome change was universally attributed to General Allenby, and that thenceforward the E.E.F. was "on him," as the phrase goes, to a man.

I wonder if many of our big commanders realised as fully as did General Allenby the enormous influence the "personal touch" had on the troops they commanded? Just to see your chief wandering about more or less informally, finding things out for himself, watching you—not on parade, but at your ordinary daily jobs; to know that he was not above getting out of his car to ask a question personally, or, during operations, to sit on a gun-limber digging his bully-beef out of a tin with a jack-knife, like any other man. These things went a mighty long way.

You get more willing and selfless service out of men if you are seen of them, known of them, and if, perhaps, you suffer with them for a space.

CHAPTER 14

The Attack on Beersheba

By the middle of October everything was ready. The railway had been brought forward as far as possible and the army at the gates of Gaza had been largely increased in numbers. That Irish Division which had had such a terrible time during the Serbian retreat in 1915 and the 60th (London) Division, which had fought both in France and Macedonia, had come from Salonica to help. There were now English, Scotch, Irish, and Welsh troops on various parts of the front; large numbers of Indian cavalry had also been added to the mounted divisions, and our artillery was at least equal, if not superior, to that of the Turks. Every scrap of transport available had been concentrated for the tremendous task of supplying the army when it began to move forward. Some idea of the magnitude of this task may be gathered from the fact that thirty thousand camels, practically the entire strength of the Camel Transport Corps, were needed for the troops on the right flank alone since they were farthest from railhead. For these it was estimated that at least a week's supply of water would have to be carried, to say nothing of forage and rations, until Beersheba with its water-supply was captured. This was to be the first part of the enterprise, and the whole plan hinged on its success.

Two divisions, one of infantry and the other of dismounted yeomanry—which latter had done so well as infantry that they were rewarded by being further employed as such—were to make for the gap between Beersheba and Sheria and make things unpleasant for the Turks occupying the defences of the former place. The part assigned to the mounted troops was that they should disappear into the desert land south-east of Beersheba and wait there till the time appointed, whereupon they were to perform the outflanking movement which, as has been stated, was utterly unforeseen by the Turks. For the moment we will, if you please, follow the fortunes of the cavalry.

If you have persevered so far with this narrative you will have noticed throughout that the troops had little assistance from Nature in beating the Turks. Here, doubtless relenting, she had with kindly forethought provided two small oases— one about twenty miles from El Chauth, the other ten miles farther away—in the desert where the cavalry was to hide. At both places there was a moderate supply of water, sufficient for a few days at any rate, which was all that was required.

During the night of October 27th, what time the Turks were being severely trounced in an attempt on the branch railway, two columns of cavalry started for these providential hiding-places, following substantially the same route as that taken when the railway between Beersheba and El Auja was blown up. The dust was still there, in greater quantities than ever after six months of drought, and the fond illusion that we had taken most of it on our persons during the railway raid was rudely shattered. Fortunately the Turks were profoundly ignorant of the move, and the two columns reached their respective destinations without discovery. They remained unseen until the night of the 30th, when the long trek northwards began. If you can imagine a mighty column of dust well over ten miles in length, in the midst of which were many thousands of half-suffocated men and horses, you have no need of further words to picture that night's march, which lasted for ten hours.

At dawn all the troops were in their assigned positions. The infantry had marched all night and were to open the performance as soon as it was light enough for the gunners to get on to their targets. At the outset these consisted of the barbed-wire entanglements with which the defences south of Beersheba were surrounded. Unfortunately the light was not too good for accurate shooting, and although most of the wire was destroyed a few patches were left which caused considerable trouble to infantry when they went forward to the assault. Moreover the Turkish—or rather Austrian—artillery fire was very heavy and accurate; they had the range of every spot in the vicinity of their defences, which our own guns found very difficult to locate. Despite the volume of fire the storming-parties pressed on, tearing down the wire with their hands or forcing themselves through it, until at last they got to close quarters with the bayonet. After that nothing could stop them, and by the early afternoon all the defences south of Beersheba had been taken. Also, the artillery by admirable shooting had succeeded in putting the railway out of action: a great feat.

By this time the Turks had received a rude shock from another direction: east-north-east. Our cavalry, having unseen closed the northern exits from the town, suddenly swooped down and seized positions menacing the town from the east. Here some topographical details will be necessary. The only way to approach Beersheba from the desert is by crossing the steep-sided Wadi es Saba—from which the town and a small village near by take their names. On the Beersheba side of the *wadi* and forming almost a semi-circle round the town is a broad, flat plain commanding which was Tel es Saba, the highest of all the surrounding hills. This had to be captured before any direct attack on the town could be made.

All day long the Australians, on foot, made desperate attempts to carry the hill by storm, but the Turks, well served by their magnificent position, held on stubbornly. Another party of the Australians scrambled across the *wadi* and made an attempt to cross the plain in face of the appalling fire that was poured into

them. They did succeed in capturing Saba villag[e]
place was a death-trap after it was taken. Just be[fore]
es Saba succumbed to the incessant hammering
all day, and one great obstacle was removed fro[m]

But fundamentally we were "no forrader. [...]
outlying positions had been taken Beersheba itself was stin
intact, and its immediate capture was urgently necessary; the
whole adventure turned upon it. With the coming of night,
the artillery had ceased fire, and of course no further support
could be expected from them. The town had to be taken by
direct assault with the bayonet; there was nothing else for
it. First the *wadi* had to be crossed, no easy matter, then the
plain, which was heavily trenched. The Yeomanry, who had
not been needed during the day, were ordered to tackle the
job—of course, dismounted. They did actually start from their
reserve positions, but they were forestalled. From under the
shadow of Tel es Saba a vast cloud of dust was seen sweeping over the moonlit plain. Inside it was the 4th Light Horse
Brigade, who, tired of waiting and with their usual cheerful
disregard of the conventions, had decided to take the town
themselves. Also, having had sufficient fighting on foot during
the all-day struggle for Tel es Saba, they determined that the
horses should share in the excitement.

So, using as lances their rifles with bayonets fixed, the whole
brigade—and any one else with a horse and rifle and bayonet—charged yelling upon the town. Over trenches, rifle-pits
and obstacles of all sorts they leapt and burst into Beersheba
like a tornado. The Turks were literally paralysed by the au-
dacity of the effort and made a mere travesty of resistance, in
comparison with their stubbornness during the day. It was all
over in a very short time and Beersheba was ours. The Yeomanry, astonished to find so little resistance, came in at the
death in time to help round up the large numbers of prisoners
captured by the Australians.

Speaking without the book I should say that this mounted

onet charge is without parallel in military history. It was at any rate worthy of the best traditions of Australian resourcefulness. Their motto seemed always to be: "If you haven't the right tools for a job, do it with anything that's handy and trust to the luck of the British army to pull you through." A very sound maxim, on the whole, if their headstrong adherence to it did sometimes land them in a tight corner.

It was difficult to realise in the midst of a jostling crowd of soldiers, with guns and all the impedimenta of war in the background, that once on a time old Father Abraham had lived at Beersheba with his family and developed the water-supply for his flocks. Impossible, too, to visualise the past splendours of Beersheba, as became the city on the southern border of Palestine, on the main caravan-route through the Land of Goshen, across the Sinai desert into Egypt, and through which on account of its wells, travellers for countless ages had passed on their leisurely journey south. Nowadays, it is but a collection of exaggerated mud-huts of the usual native type, with the addition of a few modern works and the railway.

Though I saw it frequently enough later on the sight of a railway-station in or near a native village always seemed strangely incongruous. Do not for a moment imagine that by railway-station I mean anything so elaborate as the merest village station at home; except at Kantara even the best and largest of ours did not rise to such heights. The platform, if there was one, was of sleepers piled almost haphazard one upon another with sand shovelled into the interstices and spread over the top. Occasionally cinders were used to form an extra hard surface; but this was a luxury. Unless a stationary train marked its presence the station was very difficult to find at all, for one bit of the railway looks very much like another at a distance. I remember a party of us trying for a long time to find one of these elusive places. We found the railway all right but the only sign of human habitation was a tiny wooden hut, almost invisible against the background of sand, towards which we made our way. A lance-corporal in the R.E. was the sole in-mate. "Where's the station, chum?" he was asked. He looked at us suspiciously for a moment.

"Don't come it over me," he said then; "yer standin' on it." And he was right; you could even see the platform if you peered about carefully.

At Beersheba the Turkish station was rather a pretentious affair, all things considered. There were quite a number of adequate buildings, most of them connected with the water-works just outside. The Turks, thanks in the first place to the fine shooting of our artillery, had had no chance of getting their rolling-stock away; and secondly, the spirited dash of the Australians had overwhelmed them before they could destroy any of it. In fact there was a train in the station, fully laden with stores and ready to start for Sheria had it been possible, when the Light Horse burst into the town.

Beersheba that night presented an indescribable spectacle. It is literally impossible to describe it, for every detail was obscured by the immense clouds of dust that hung over the place like a pall, clinging and opaque. The water-works and wells were fortunately intact, but until everything had been carefully tested and examined, the horses, who had drunk nothing since the previous day, had to remain thirsty. In the morning the town was systematically searched.

There were mines and bombs and infernal-machines eve-rywhere, all obviously made in Germany. The Turk usually limited his nefarious practices to poisoning the wells when he retreated—a sufficiently damnable thing to do, *bien entendu*. But the Germans despised crude methods of this kind. They were not content with poisoning the water but must needs fix their devilish contraptions so that a man blew himself to pieces in the act of drawing his drink. Many of the wells were mined, but the Germans had slightly overreached themselves either through haste or clumsiness, and all the mines were removed without mishap.

Elsewhere we were not so fortunate. Some of our native camel-drivers saw tins of preserved meat conspicuously lying about without owners. Following the invariable native principle of obtaining something for nothing whenever possible, one or two seized them. It is a melancholy fact that the act was their last in this world, for the tins were simply—potted death. After this men gave a wide berth even to the most innocent-looking objects, though in truth the more innocent a thing looked the more devilish was the contrivance hidden under it. Now observe further the workings of the German mind. In one dug-out there was—of all books—a copy of Ruskin's Sesame and Lilies, tattered and dog's-eared by constant use, and a torn piece of—the Sporting Times! Also, hanging on a nail in one of the beams was a German tunic, stretched neatly on a coat-hanger. The dug-out looked very innocent and had quite a domesticated atmosphere; and the unwary, lulled into security by it, might have been tempted casually to reach for the tunic as a trophy. Providentially no one pulled it down until the engineers had inspected the dug-out, and then only from the end of a very long rope. There was little left of the dug-out after the explosion.

What can you make of a mind that can appreciate and enjoy the incomparable beauty of Sesame and Lilies, and yet can conceive so hidden and treacherous a means of destruction? Of course the book might have come fortuitously into the possession of the occupant of the dug-out, might even have been left there and forgotten by some passing British soldier when the place was captured; but the latter at least is unlikely. When inquisitiveness had such dire results no one did much prying until everything had been examined and pronounced safe. But that the wells were safe was the great thing and their importance could hardly be over-estimated.

They must be amongst the oldest in the world. For thirty-seven centuries there has been water at Beersheba, since, in fact, Abraham sank the wells in the neighbourhood, and these have known many vicissitudes. When he died the Philistines came and rendered them all useless by filling them up with sand: a precedent, you will have noticed, much favoured by the Turks, though their methods were more modern. Years after came Isaac and excavated the wells again; whereupon he had to fight with the men of Gerar for the possession of them. Tiring of strife he dug the well at Beersheba which gives the town its name, and this he retained, having made peace with the Philistines. Finally, history repeating itself nearly four thousand years later, British soldiers fought for, and won, these self-same wells, which were substantially in as good condition as when they were first made.

But what had been an ample supply for the flocks of the patriarchs and passing caravans proved inadequate for the needs of the thousands of men and horses and camels thronging into Beersheba. A hundred thousand gallons is a big tax on the capacity of any well, and this is a very moderate estimate of the amount required daily by the troops. From the moment they were pronounced fit for use the watering-places by the station were crowded with thirsty men and animals, and the supply soon decreased alarmingly. To add to the trouble most of the stored water, accumulated previously with such care and labour, was delayed somewhere en route to Beersheba and ultimately had considerable difficulty in reaching the place at all. Meanwhile the "Cameliers," whose mounts could last in fair comfort for a week without water, went off into the parched hills north of Beersheba to perform their usual function of protecting our flank. Then all the mounted troops took the road towards Sheria, so as to be in readiness for the main blow when the transport difficulty had been solved.

Chapter 15

Gaza at Last

During the days immediately following the capture of Beersheba the mounted troops were kept exceedingly busy, for our position was yet by no means secure. Every day the Turks in the hills made an attempt to drive us eastwards into the desert and every day we strove to push them back on to their defences at Sheria. It was a series of battles for the wells, in effect, for here the eternal problems of transport and water were acute. The former was more or less solved in time for the big operations; the latter was the difficulty it had always been for the past two years, but in a different way. In the desert, whilst the wells were few and far between they were seldom more than fifty or sixty feet deep; in the district around Beersheba there were, to exaggerate a little, almost as many wells as in the whole of the Sinai Desert, but you could not get at the water! Scarcely a well was less than a hundred feet deep and most of them were anything over that up to a hundred and eighty; of course there were no pumps. The old *shadouf* of the desert, unwieldy though it was, would have been a veritable godsend to the troops here.

A cavalryman could not pack a two-hundred foot coil of the lightest rope on to his saddle; it was as much as he could do to climb into it over the conglomeration of picketing-pegs and ropes, rifle-bucket, and sword which constituted his full marching order, and it was more or less the same in the artillery.

Those patriarchs of old who built the wells would doubt-less have been vastly diverted to see a trooper sit down and solemnly remove his putties with which to lengthen a "rope" already consisting of reins, belts, and any odds and ends of rope he had acquired, and when even these additions proved insufficient—! It was a joke which matured but slowly.

Imagine half a brigade of cavalry clustered round a well frantically devising means to reach the cavernous depths, while the other half were fighting like tigers to keep off the Turks a few miles away! It was nothing out of the ordinary for a squadron or battery to take five hours to water their horses; and it added a piquancy to the situation that you were never quite sure when a marauding party of Turks would appear over the top of a neighbouring hill. Ultimately the extraordinary exertions of the engineers saved the situation; with incredible labour and ingenuity they fixed pumping-appliances to the wells. They must have used most of the kinds known to science, and assuredly a great many not in the textbooks. In the course of their work they performed the functions of a hundred trades—including divers: in fact a large part of their time was of necessity spent in the water, and a singularly unpleasant business it must have been, dangling for hours at the end of a rope in the dank atmosphere of a well. Practically everything had to be done in the first two days after the capture of Beersheba in order to secure our precarious hold on that place; and with the lack of quick transport—for the country was too rough for motors, and camels are very slow—the shortage of rope and appliances, with, in fine, everything against them, the engineers in successfully accomplishing the feat added one more to their already imposing list of miracles.

Let there be no mistake about it; it was a miracle and one performed only by the most complete abnegation of self. Men who doubtless would have groused at home had they been asked to work for a couple of hours overtime at bank or office or works, here slaved for twenty-four hours at a stretch without bite or sup, and then after a short rest went on for another twenty-four. It is astonishing what the human frame can be made to do, when it is driven by that indescribable thing variously called morale or esprit de corps or duty.

The same feeling of superb confidence in the outcome animated the whole army, from the men clinging tenaciously to Beersheba to those straining impatiently at the leash in front of Gaza. The turn of the latter came on November 1st, and the account of their exploits must be taken from official sources, since by some inexplicable oversight on the part of Nature, a man cannot be in two places at once.

According to General Allenby's dispatches, it was decided to make a strong attack on some of the ridges defending Gaza, for the purpose chiefly of preventing the enemy from sending reinforcements or reserves across to the other flank. Also, any gains would be of material assistance when the time came for striking the big blow in the centre. The first part of the attack was made by the Scotch division on Umbrella Hill, previously mentioned in this narrative as being the scene of a raid by the same troops in the middle of June. Just before sunset the artillery put up a tremendous bombardment which lasted until dusk, and shortly before midnight the Scotsmen attacked the hill. To many of them it must have been reminiscent of their desperate assault on Wellington Ridge, during one phase of the battle of Romani, for Umbrella Hill was somewhat similarly shaped and the approach to it was over a wide expanse of heavy, yielding sand. But here the Turks were partially taken by surprise, and the Jocks were amongst them and had bundled them out of their trenches almost before they knew, though as usual they fought desperately hard once they were alive to the situation. Thus the first part of the enterprise was safely accomplished with comparatively little loss; the second and more difficult attempt began before daylight the next morning. The main objective was Sheikh Hassan, a ridge sloping gently down to the Mediterranean north-west of Gaza. This was nearly two miles from the nearest British trenches, and the ground to be covered by the attacking infantry was of the rough and difficult nature characteristic of this part of the coast. The artillery, including the heavy guns of the battleships off the coast, kept up an intense barrage while the troops were in the open, and, in addition to knocking the trenches on Sheikh Hassan out of shape, completely destroyed some works nearer Gaza. With these as a foothold the infantry stormed the main position with the bayonet, though the Turkish machine-gun fire was deadly and their resistance stubborn in the extreme. But this was the opportunity of "getting a little of their own back" for which our men, especially the 52nd and 54th Divisions, had been waiting for six months, and it was more than the Turks could do to keep them out.

Besides, Sheikh Hassan was no more than the *hors d'oeuvre* to the feast, so to speak, and it was swallowed with gusto. In this action, for the first time, I believe, the French and Italians assisted the British on land as well as from the sea. It was also the last occasion on which the Baby Tanks were used, for in the subsequent fighting amongst the Judean hills the country was too rough even for the larger specimens successfully to have negotiated.

Of the important defences in the immediate neighbourhood of Gaza, only grim old Ali Muntar now remained unconquered, and still reared a defiant head above his humbler satellites. As was fitting, and indeed very necessary, its capture was left till the last. Meanwhile, the preliminaries being completed more or less successfully, the main blow at the centre had to be struck. During the night of November 5th the great move toward Sheria was begun, and by the morning all the troops were in the positions assigned to them. The principal Turkish position was on Kauwukah Ridge, as usual very difficult to approach and positively crawling with machine-guns and wire. As was a customary feature with the Turkish defences, if one position was captured it could immediately be enfiladed from another portion; and very little was left to chance to make the place secure.

The 74th Division attacked the eastern and more vulnerable end first, and with such amazing élan did they fight—and it was all the more remarkable in that these troops were dismounted Yeomanry—that by the early afternoon they had swept the Turks out of their trenches in this part of Kauwukah, and were firmly established in what remained of the position. At the other end of the ridge two more divisions were fighting towards a maze of wire, which was rapidly being uprooted by the accurate and devastating fire of our artillery. This was the heaviest bombardment of the battle; some of the Turkish trenches were simply swept out of existence, and the defenders irretrievably buried in the debris. One of the attacking divisions was Irish, who as a pleasing change from road-making in that malarial hole, Salonica, gave of their best with the bayonet, in which bright pastime they were capably aided and abetted by the 60th Division. It is the fashion to speak of successful military operations as being carried out "like clockwork." If extreme dash and gallantry in the face of every obstacle that brain of man could devise constitute the "clockwork," then the attack that led to the capture of Kauwukah Ridge merits the above description.

I cannot write of the attack as an eye-witness but, months afterwards, I saw the Turkish system of defences, and little imagination was needed to picture the terrible struggle it must have been to take them by storm.

Late in the afternoon the two divisions had captured all their objectives as far as, and including, Sheria railway-station. On the right flank, too, where success was no less important, the troops had done their share; and here in the hills north of Beersheba the fighting was terribly severe. It is one thing to attack with numbers at least equal, if not superior, to those of the enemy; it is quite another when the advantage of numbers lies heavily with the enemy, and the attack has still to be made. This was the predicament in which the Welshmen found themselves; they had not only to prevent themselves from being cut off, but had to drive a vastly superior force out of commanding positions they had taken, and not all the hammering of the Turks could oust them permanently. It was attack and counter-attack from one hill to another all day long, but the advantage at the end of the day lay with the Welshmen, who simply refused to be beaten and fought the Turks to a standstill. Like the Scotsmen they had to wipe off a few old scores, in addition to which there was the accumulated interest of six months of waiting.

By these operations Gaza was isolated except from the north but, as the Turks had no more reserves immediately available, little danger was to be feared from that direction. During the night the Turkish commander, seeing that the game was up, skilfully evacuated all the defences of Gaza, with the exception of those at Atawina Ridge, from which, as will be seen by a glance at the map, the defenders could best protect his rear from the onslaught of the victorious troops advancing from the east. There was no necessity, therefore, for an assault on Ali Muntar; its deserted slopes were occupied without opposition the next day. It thus remained unconquered to the end, and no one begrudged the barren victory, for many thousands of British lives were saved in consequence. By the time Gaza was occupied by our troops, the remaining Turkish defences except Atawina had fallen into our hands. This, too, was evacuated when the garrison had done their work of delaying our advance and protecting the main retreating body. It was due to their dogged defence that a larger number of prisoners were not taken by the British, and the two almost bloodless retirements were admittedly very ably carried out.

Thus, in six days the patient labours of six months had on the one hand been brought to nought, and on the other had been crowned by complete success. The fall of Gaza gave us the key to the whole of the Maritime plain of Palestine. It was one of the five great cities of the Philistines, and the only one that had retained even a degree of its former greatness; with the others the cry is "Ichabod!"

Of the town itself it is unnecessary to say more than that while there are several fine modern buildings, amongst them a German school, and a mosque which had suffered from our shells on account of the Turkish persistence in using it as an observation post, the greater part of the town is like every other Eastern town in its utter disregard of the elementary laws of sanitation. The white roofs in a ring of cactus and amid the scarlet blossoms of the pomegranate make a delightful picture seen from the top of a neighbouring hill, but there is the usual complete disillusionment when you have passed the outskirts of the town. Not all the dirt and squalor, however, could minimise the intense feeling of satisfaction amongst the troops at having at last conquered the bogy that had for so long prevented the advance into the Holy Land.

As usual the Turks did as much damage as they could before leaving. The more pretentious houses had scarcely anything of value left in them; their owners and, in fact, all the chiefs of the native population of Gaza had long since been deported. Most of these were grossly ill-treated, and some had been hanged, for what crime other than a desire to live at peace with their neighbours only the criminals who executed them knew.

It took many weeks of labour before the engineers could repair the damage done to the water-supply, which, in and around Gaza, was fairly ample. But now, the Turks having been driven out of their strongholds, it was necessary to keep them on the move northwards, to fight them whenever they could be brought to the sticking-point and to harass them night and day. After six months of comparative stagnation the troops were ready, and more than willing for operations of this nature. They wanted a little moving warfare for a change, and General Allenby supplied the need.

When the capture of the Turkish Lines was complete, the whole Army was ordered to advance, and for the next fortnight the pursuit never slackened. The story would fill a volume could you collect but half of the incidents of those stirring days. It was an epic of endurance and utter indifference to hardship. Few men, however, could tell a connected tale of what happened, for, obedient to the command, the enemy was attacked whenever he was encountered, which was every day.

The Turks were beaten, but they were by no means demoralised. On all parts of the front our advance was stubbornly resisted. On our left flank they fought with most bitter determination to save their railhead for long enough to get their guns and stores away, and having succeeded in doing this retired farther up the coast and prepared to fight again. On our right flank the mounted divisions, who had started from Beersheba on the night Gaza was evacuated to perform their usual function of cutting off the enemy's retreat, were assaulted vigorously by a strong rearguard of Turks who fought in anything but a beaten manner. It was here that the Yeomanry made a charge reminiscent of the charge of the Light Brigade at Balaclava.

There was no blunder about this charge, however, which was made in face of point-blank fire from "5.9's" and other guns, all of which were captured. It is no more than bare justice to say that the Austrian gunners gallantly stuck to their guns till the Yeomanry swept through them and cut them down where they stood.

Later, the Yeomanry had further opportunities of which they availed themselves to the full; they, too, had a few painful memories to wipe out. After the occupation of Huj, where the Turks had an enormous depot, the pursuit quickened, as could be seen by the increasing litter of stores the enemy left behind. Some idea of the amount of material used in a modern battle may be gathered from the fact that one of our cable-sections salved forty thousand pounds' worth of copper wire alone, all of which had been employed on the battlefield.

Infantry and mounted troops marched and fought to their utmost capacity, ignoring their hardships. Rations arrived—when they arrived, and some days they came not at all. If there were but four men to share in one tin of bully-beef or one pound of biscuits they counted themselves fortunate. Almost every man carried a "billy" slung on to the hook at the back of his tunic, a habit learnt from the Australians. This was generally made out of an empty fruit tin, with a piece of wire for a handle. Perhaps the drivers of one team would have one billy-can, the genuine article, between them, and this is large enough to hold about four mugs of tea.

The scarcity of wood was a great difficulty. Every man in the team was strictly enjoined to "scrounge" any scrap of wood he could find en route, and it was a common sight to see a driver suddenly hop off his horse, dart across the road triumphantly to seize a stick he had spotted, after which he rushed after his team and scrambled into the saddle again, the horses meanwhile plodding patiently along. Then, the moment word of a halt for a quarter of an hour came down the long line, every man in the team quickly dismounted and a toll of sticks was collected from each by the "cook." Then the billy was placed precariously on the heap and in a few minutes you would see the tiny fires all along the column.

What wonderful tea that was! In hot countries there is no drink to equal it, either taken scalding hot to prevent heat apoplexy or as cold as you can get it, without milk or sugar, to be carried in your water-bottle. Many a man was saved from collapse by a timely mug of hot tea, and if there was a rum ration to go with it, so much the better.

But, alas, one of the essentials for making tea was often lacking; the farther we advanced the scarcer did water become, and now there were no pumps to draw it from the wells. Horses went three days and more without drinking, and hundreds died from thirst and exhaustion. Infantry, starting with empty water-bottles, marched thirty miles across country, with a bayonet-charge thrown in, and found perhaps a pint of water per man at the end of the day.

Then the rain came. Roads, at best no more than a travesty of the name and already battered by Turkish transport, became quagmires of mud through which artillery-horses, weakened by thirst and meagre rations, could scarcely draw the guns. The transport, toiling along in the rear, had the utmost difficulty in bringing up supplies, and as for the men, they were unwashed, unshaven, and covered with mud from head to foot.

Through all the strongholds of the Philistines, through villages with historic names the army passed as the line of pursuit swung north-westwards across the plain of Philistia. Past ruined Ascalon on the coast; Mejdel, farther inland, one of the largest native towns on the plain, with many ancient industries established there; Esdud, the ancient Ashdod, where later a station on the military railway was built; Gath, where the Turks made a most desperate attempt to delay our advance; Akron, the once great frontier fortress of the Philistines; these were among the chief. In addition there were modern Jewish colonies, depleted of their male inhabitants but otherwise untouched, where a kind of coarse red wine was obtained which helped greatly to ward off ill-effects from cold and wet.

At last, after five days of hot pursuit, the Turks made a last great stand in defence of the junction between the Jerusalem railway and the main line, and also of Et Tineh, which connected the Gaza and Beersheba railway. The Yeomanry, acting with the Scotch infantry, distinguished themselves in the action for possession of the former, taking the main Turkish position after a wild gallop for a couple of miles under heavy fire all the way.

The Light Horse captured Et Tineh and a host of prisoners besides. Everywhere the Turks were forced back. Their army was cut in two, one half retiring on Jerusalem, the other going north towards Jaffa. In their efforts to speed the heels of the former the Yeomanry again made a wonderful charge against a high hill, a few miles from Latron on the Jerusalem Road, strongly defended by the Turks. It is an unusual feat for cavalry even to attack a hill of considerable dimensions, but the Yeomanry not only did this but galloped to the top of it and killed or captured all the defenders. Yet at the beginning of the War there were people who said that the day of cavalry was over! The campaign in Egypt and Palestine was one long and continued refutation of this view.

On November 15th British troops occupied Lydda, or Ludd, as it was afterwards called, which town, according to legend, contains the tomb of our patron-saint St. George. With the capture of Jaffa the next day, the advance for the moment ended.

CHAPTER 16

The Road to Jerusalem

Since the fall of Beersheba the twentieth-century Crusaders had marched and fought across one-third of the most famous battle-ground in all history. It is a melancholy and ironic fact that this land, hallowed by the gentle footsteps of the Prince of Peace, has seen more bloodshed than any country on the earth. There is scarcely a village from Dan even unto Beersheba which has not been the scene of desperate carnage at some time or other in its history; and around Jerusalem the hills and valleys have run with blood at any time these four thousand years.

Across these valleys and into these hills climbed the British cavalry, for though Jaffa, the most considerable port in Palestine, had been captured and held, a greater objective was in view.

All roads now led to Jerusalem. This expression, let me hasten to add, is merely figurative. The exasperating fact was, that all roads did not lead to Jerusalem; most of them led nowhere except over a precipice; and they were but glorified goat-tracks at best. You needed the agility of a monkey, the leaping powers of a "big-horn" and the lungs of a Marathon runner successfully to negotiate them. Moreover, by some oversight, the authorities had neglected to provide the troops with alpenstocks. Without these adventitious aids the cavalry penetrated the northern defiles of the hills, following substantially the route taken by all the ancient invaders from the north. Before the disorganised Turks were fully alive to their advance they had reached the historic pass of Beth-Horon.

Through here that picturesque Assyrian warrior Sennacherib must have passed when he "came down like a wolf on the fold; and his cohorts were gleaming in purple and gold." It is to be hoped that the invasion did not take place in the rainy season or the cohorts would have been sadly bedraggled before they had reached Michmash. It will be remembered by most as the scene of Joshua's passionate exhortation: *"Sun, stand thou still upon Gibeon; and Thou, Moon, in the Valley of Ajalon,"* on that day when, having defeated the Amorites with great slaughter, he was fearful lest night should fall before he could turn the defeat into a rout. It must have been a wonderful and uplifting day for the Israelites, after so many years of oppression. Through Beth-Horon, twenty-five centuries later, passed our own Richard Coeur de Lion on his last crusade; when, finding to his bitter mortification that his forces were so depleted by disease and death that he could not go on, he turned his back and refused even to look upon the City he could not save.

After which brief incursion into the past let us return to history in the making, not that the cavalry as a whole troubled themselves greatly about anything so high-falutin'. Their immediate concern was to maintain their precarious foothold in these melancholy hills; and if they worried at all it was over the important question as to whether rations in satisfactory quantities could be brought to them. With complete unanimity they cursed the mist-like rain that shut out the surrounding hills from view; for they, together with the whole army, had bitter reason for mistrusting fog, after Katia and the first battle of Gaza.

Despite increasing pressure from the Turks, now awake to the seriousness of their position, the cavalry held on to their positions and even advanced a little, so affording the necessary protection for the advance of the infantry farther to the south. These were marching on Jerusalem from the British positions at Ludd and Ramleh, which latter place had been Turkish G.H.Q.

From the west to Jerusalem there is but one road which can properly be described as such, but it is one of the most travelled roads in the world, and certainly amongst the most famous. In every age and from all countries thousands of pilgrims landing at Jaffa have trodden this ancient road to the Holy City. The first part of it is indescribably beautiful, leading as it does through some of the orange groves which surround Jaffa. In the springtime, if you turn your horse a mile or two away from the town an incomparable view is spread before your eyes. On every hand stretch the orange groves, great splashes of white and green, the scent from which is almost overpoweringly sweet. Here and there you see the darker green of the olive and the blazing scarlet of the pomegranate blossom, divided into patches by hedges of prickly pear; and scattered about promiscuously are oleanders, cypresses, and the stately sycamores. In the midst of it all lies Jaffa the Beautiful, almost virginal in its whiteness, and beyond, in almost incredible harmony of colour, the purple waters of the Mediterranean.

Across the southern end of the Plain of Sharon the road leads through cultivated fields, past vineyards and orchards, as far as Ramleh, where the somewhat monotonous beauty of the plain ends abruptly. Some miles beyond, the road, at the time the infantry advance was made, had degenerated into a cart-track from the battering it had received from Turkish traffic.

About ten miles from Ramleh was Latron, a malaria-haunted swamp in the rainy season and a plague-spot of flies in summer, and from here onwards the road became increasingly difficult and dismal. You could see the imprint of the oppressor in the very land itself, for though there are a few patches of cultivation, the greater part of the countryside is abandoned to a stony barrenness. The first check to the infantry came at Bab el Wad, a rocky, desolate pass, which, had the Turks been allowed time properly to fortify it, would have held up the advance and delayed the fall of Jerusalem probably for months. As it was they fought desperately hard to retain it, but having come so far in their pilgrimage, the infantry did not allow this obstacle to stand in their way and carried the pass at the point of the bayonet. After which spirited effort they proceeded onwards as far as Enab, the "Hill of Grapes," a beautiful little place some six miles from Jerusalem where later a Desert Corps Rest Camp was established. Here the advance for the moment ended.

In the midst of the hills and valleys between the position of the infantry and that of the cavalry near Beth-Horon towered the hill called Nebi Samwil, the highest point in Palestine. This was a great serried mass of rock rising by sharp degrees to a height of nearly 3000 feet, where the infantry in some places had to sling their rifles and pull themselves up by their hands, during their successful attack on the ridge. This kind of alpine-climbing-cum-fighting was as different from the fighting on the desert as it could well be, and only the infantryman, who did most of it, could tell you which he detested the more. As one of them said, in the Judean hills you were mountaineer, pack-mule, and soldier all in one; and it is not for a mere helpless artilleryman to paint the lily.

When Nebi Samwil had been captured and consolidated the whole line took root, as it were, and prepared to beat off the increasingly violent attacks of the Turks, while the engineers started to improve the roads and other means of communication. The railway had to be brought up from Belah, no easy task in the rainy season; for if laying the line across the desert had been difficult, it was infinitely worse building it from Belah across the Shephaleh to the British line. The Wadi Ghuzzee was a raging torrent by now, and even a few miles from its mouth the turbulent waters were a constant source of worry and anxiety to the engineers. I believe I am right in saying that three times in the winter months was the bridge over the *wadi* washed away by the floods, and each time the engineers had incredible difficulty in building it up again. While it was down all traffic beyond Belah was necessarily suspended and troops coming up the line from Kantara were often three weeks on the journey to their respective units.

Frequently enough when men did at last arrive at their destinations it was only to find that their battery or battalion had moved to some other part of the front, generally with an unpronounceable name of which nobody had ever heard! Few things are more wearisome than searching for a unit in such a country as Palestine, especially in that part which comprises the Judean hills. Men coming up from the base in those winter months were often given three, four, and sometimes six days' rations, so difficult was it for a man to reach his unit.

The Turkish railway from Beit Hanun relieved the pressure to some extent, when the damage it had suffered from our shells had been made good. The only way it could be used was in conjunction with the mercantile marine, who landed stores on to the beach as they had done at Belah before the second battle of Gaza. One such landing-place was at Wadi Sukerier, a bleak, inhospitable swamp north of Ascalon, where a great dump was established in the mud, the supplies from which were transported north by camel convoys. The great obstacles in the way of landing stores from ships were the extremely dangerous coast and enemy submarines. The Mediterranean, as elsewhere, was alive with "U" boats in the summer and autumn of 1917. They levied a heavy toll on "troopers" and supply-ships coming out East, and the Navy in its work of guarding the coast of Palestine during the landing of supplies did not escape unscathed. That this was carried on successfully and the troops in the Judean hills were fed was very largely owing to the untiring vigilance of British and Allied monitors and destroyers.

The port of Jaffa was also used, and here the conditions were even worse. Strictly speaking Jaffa is a port only in name, for all vessels have to anchor off-shore and passengers and stores have to be landed in surf-boats. In the rainy season the bar is almost impassable four days in the week and the roar of the breakers can be heard miles away. Even when the sea was calm enough for stores to be landed, the ground swell was such as to make the ordinary landsman agree with Dr. Johnson's remark "that he would rather go to gaol than to sea." It is easy to understand why the materials for Solomon's Temple were brought to Jaffa on rafts; no other craft of those days would have withstood the buffetings of the breakers.

But why Jonah ever chose this place from which to start his long journey to Tarshish passes my comprehension unless, indeed, it was Hobson's choice. He must certainly have been violently ill ere ever his flimsy boat had crossed the bar—a feat his whale could never have accomplished at all—and for a man of his temperament, soured by many trials, this must have been the last straw.

Patience, by the way, was a powerful characteristic of the sailors engaged in landing stores on the coast. A supply-ship, finding the sea at the Wadi Sukerier too high to permit of stores being landed, went on to Jaffa, found the breakers impossibly high there and returned to Sukerier. This amusing pastime went on for three days, when the waters abated somewhat and the stores were safely landed. As there was a "U" boat in the offing most of the time, however, the humour of the situation did not strike the sailors till afterwards.

Such were some of the difficulties confronting those who were responsible for supplying the army with rations; and those whose business it was to carry them to the troops holding the line could tell a similar story. Although the engineers made roads where none had previously existed, and blew the side out of a cliff in order to improve one already in use, the lot of the transport services, and more particularly of the "Camels," was not a happy one. Everything was against them, especially the weather. Rain and cold are the camels' worst enemies, and thousands perished of exposure, but the work still went on at all hours of the day and night, in all weathers, and over every imaginable kind of road but a good one.

Troops holding outlying positions in the hills were inaccessible to any form of transport but camels, and these had frequently to climb up steep, rocky paths just wide enough to take them and their burdens. On the one side was a precipice; on the other an abyss. Each camel-driver usually led a couple of camels, marching abreast, but when the narrowness of the path made it necessary for them to climb in single file, one was tied by his head-rope to the rear of the other camel's saddle. This, though it was absolutely necessary, rather added to the dangers of the climb. The incessant rains had made the paths slippery in the extreme, and the camel at the best of times is not the most adaptable of creatures; his conformation, moreover, is all against him in so far as scaling a cliff is concerned.

The merest slip on one of these treacherous paths meant destruction. The rear-most camel would stumble, oscillate violently for a moment, and over the side he would go, probably dragging his fellow with him and not infrequently the unfortunate driver as well. Sometimes a camel out of pure cussedness would "barrack" in the middle of a precipitous, narrow path, and only by crawling through the legs of the halted camels could he be reached by the exasperated officer or N.C.O. in charge of the party.

Now a camel has all the obstinacy of a mule and, in addition, is almost impervious to pain. Flogging has little effect on him and profanity none whatever; violence is necessary. Frequently the only way to shift one of these obstinate beasts was by lighting a fire under him! Then he moved, sometimes in such a hurry that he fell over the precipice and broke his neck. I am aware that this method is not mentioned in Field Service Regulations, but a great many things are done on active service which do not come within the scope of that admirable volume. Further, when men's lives were dependent on their receiving food and water at stated times, any methods were justifiable. You could not stop the War and wait till one recalcitrant camel was ready to allow six hundred of his fellows to pass on their lawful occasions.

I speak not without some small personal experience of the vagaries of the camel, though fortunately I was never driven to the extreme measures described above, for some time before the operations about Jerusalem began I retired to "another place" via a *cacolet*-camel and the hospital train; and when I again emerged it was in another guise and under the aegis of the "Camels."

This must also be my excuse for omitting further details of the fall of Jerusalem; but as this part of the campaign at least attained the fullest publicity and has already been described by many more capable pens than mine, the omission need cause the reader no loss of rest. I would say, however, that the deliverance of the Holy City after four centuries of Turkish tyranny and oppression was the signal for extraordinary rejoicing amongst the Jews not only in Jerusalem but all over Egypt. General Allenby's unassuming entry, on foot, into the Holy City and his assurance that every man might worship without let or hindrance according to the tenets of the religion in which he believed, whether Christian or Mussulman, profoundly impressed the inhabitants and made the whole proceedings a triumph for British diplomacy and love of freedom. Moreover, our prestige, which for three years had been at a very low ebb, by the capture of Jerusalem leapt at one bound to a height never before attained in Egypt, always a country of sedition and intrigue.

Finally, to the notice of those interested in prophecy, I would commend the following:

Blessed is he that waiteth and cometh to the thousand three hundred and thirty-five days.

Book of Daniel, chap, xii., verse 12

Jerusalem fell in the year 1335 of the Hegira, which is 1917 in the Christian Era.

CHAPTER 17

Où l'on S'amuse

If I set out to make a categorical list of the things that existed or were made for our amusement in Palestine, it would, I think, consist of no more than four items, viz.: sea-bathing, military sports, sight-seeing, and concert parties; and I am not sure that the last-named ought to be included, for it was not until the final year of the campaign that they played any considerable part. Certainly Palestine was a difficult country in which to set up any of the more usual forms of relaxation. There were no neat little towns just behind the lines where a man could drink his glass of beer while he sat and watched the pictures, for example; nor were the Judean hills exactly the ideal place wherein to set up a cinema or theatre of your own. Those who were fortunate enough to be stationed near Jaffa could, of course, visit that delectable spot, with its glorious surroundings and incredibly filthy streets; where they could see the alleged house of Simon the Tanner, or tread the sands whereon Napoleon slaughtered some three thousand prisoners in cold blood because he had no idea what else to do with them; and where, if they had a mind to renew the agony of their schooldays, they could pick out the extremely common-place rocks to which that unfortunate lady Andromeda was chained before her sensational rescue by Perseus.

These about exhausted the amusements of Jaffa, and you will notice that they do not exactly make for hilarity. A few miles away to the south were the Jewish colonies at Richon and Duran, whose inhabitants were extremely hospitable, and any troops quartered there subsequent to the fall of Jerusalem were assured of a warm welcome. At the former there was a considerable vine-growing industry and, as a natural concomitant, the troops showed commendable industry in drinking the produce.

Personally, I remember Richon chiefly because a tragedy befell me there. The village contained a real barber's shop, if one may judge from the word *Coiffeur* writ large on the sign outside, and having heard of this startling phenomenon I rode over one evening for a hair-cut and shampoo. My foot was on the very threshold when a large person clad in fine raiment and wearing an armlet inscribed with the mystic letters "A.P.M." emerged from the shop, banged the door and pinned thereon a notice: "Out of Bounds." I pointed dramatically to my tangled mop of hair. "Eight weeks," I murmured brokenly. Whether or no that young man thought I was repeating the name of an erotic novel I cannot say, but he made a very tactless answer. I retired discomfited to find that my camel, having succeeded in breaking his head-rope, had returned to home and friends, leaving me to trudge back to camp and the tender mercies of the horse-clippers. I never heard for what crime the barber had been arraigned, though it would appear that the word *Coiffeur* can be sometimes misinterpreted; but I find it hard to forgive the A.P.M. for not allowing him to continue in his nefarious career, whatever it was, for another quarter of an hour. Successfully to cut your own hair needs, I imagine, considerable agility and a complicated arrangement of mirrors; and a pair of horse-clippers, the only alternative, was a fearsome weapon in the hands of a man whose sole experience in the hair-cutting profession was a murderous performance every morning with an army razor.

Elsewhere on the western portion of the front there were one or two similar small towns, but either they were out of bounds for sanitary reasons or were negligible in the matter of amusement; the average native village offered no inducement whatever for a visit. Even Ludd, which in the spring and summer of 1918 became a mighty depot and the terminus of the Military Railway for the time being, never rose to the dignity of a cinema. Like the inhabitants of a certain country village in the North of England, if you wanted distraction at Ludd you went to the station and watched the trains shunt. After the Turks had made the last of a series of costly but abortive counter-attacks to regain Jerusalem and were finally and for ever driven back, the city was placed strictly out of bounds until Borton Pasha and the medical authorities had thoroughly purged it of all unpleasantness: the Germans and Turks were extremely unclean in their habits. Later, when this had been done, Desert Corps established a Rest Camp at Enab, about six miles from Jerusalem, and from time to time organised parties to visit the tombs and other holy places in the neighbourhood. As these were very well arranged and were usually in charge of padres from the various denominations they were much appreciated by the tired men coming up from the Jordan Valley for a rest. It is no part of my purpose to take the reader on a kind of personally conducted war-time tour of Jerusalem; the guide books will supply him with all the information he wants. Besides, he would inevitably be disappointed, unless his first glimpse of the Holy City was from the summit of Nebi Samwil or, coming out of the Jordan Valley on a moonlit night, he saw the shimmering radiance of the Mosque of Omar at the top of Mount Moriah.

But the Rest Camp at Enab was strictly limited both in size and scope. It was for the use of the mounted divisions only, and men went there chiefly for a rest; amusement, such as could be had in the form of sight-seeing, was of secondary importance. A more universal camp was at Beni Saleh, on the coast near Khan Yunus, where glorious sea-bathing was to be had; it was, in fact, the only thing to do.

You started the day by a wild sprint across the short stretch of beach between the tents and the sea, finishing up with a headlong dash into the water, which was just cold enough to make the body tingle, but imparted none of the shock that comes with the morning tub at home. This gave you an appetite for breakfast, if any such aid were needed. When the sun grew hot towards the middle of the morning you went in the sea again and stayed there for an hour or two, with an occasional sprawl on the warm sand by way of a sun-bath.

If you felt particularly energetic a pair of ancient drill shorts rolled up and tied with a piece of a head-rope made quite an adequate ball for water-polo, until it became water-logged and sank to the bottom; then you had to fish it out and spread it on the sands until it was dry enough to resume duty. A few units used footballs for water-polo, but this was mere luxury. Ours, worse luck, always had a puncture somewhere in its internal economy.

Another camp on a similar but larger scale was the attractively named "Change of Air" Camp at El Arish, which could accommodate some thousands of men at a time. Here the tents were pitched almost at the water's edge. Men divided their day between lounging about in their pyjamas and bathing, whilst in the evening they could sit and listen to one of the numerous concert parties who came up the line from Egypt. There was also a library of sorts; it was, rather, an *olla podrida* of books, some left by the troops themselves, but largely cast-offs from the stately homes of England, ranging in variety from the admirable racing-stories of Mr. Nat Gould to a learned treatise on bee-keeping, the latter evidently intended by the sender as a guide to budding colonists in the Land of Canaan.

Many thousands of the troops in Palestine will, I fancy, have pleasant memories of these two camps, if only because you could, if you wished, bathe for twenty-four hours every day; and it was a wonderful sensation to feel really clean.

Those who had the misfortune to sojourn for a while at Deir Sineid, however, will remember the Rest Camp there with quite different feelings.

This was established during the rainy season of 1917-18, and most of the rain in Palestine fell on the Rest Camp. Troops returning from Kantara to rejoin the Desert Corps stopped at Deir Sineid en route. Sometimes, more particularly when the railway was flooded, the congestion was so great that one tent to sixteen men was considered a liberal allowance by the authorities. The men thought otherwise. Once the sixteen were safely wedged in, there they stopped for the night. There was, indeed, no encouragement to wander abroad even if you could get out without the aid of a shoe-horn.

Frequently a tent collapsed under the weight of its responsibilities, and there are few things more disconcerting to a sleeping man than suddenly to be enveloped in a mass of cold, clammy canvas. Mr. Jerome, in *Three Men in a Boat*, speaks amusingly of his efforts at putting up a tent; by the same token, his description as an onlooker of the efforts of sixteen sleepy but infuriated soldiers, indifferently protected by a ground-sheet against the cold blast and the pouring rain, struggling to erect a tent in ankle-deep mud would have been deliriously comic. One party acquired a number of wooden boxes—once the home of tins of "Ideal" milk—with which to make a floor for their tent. This answered satisfactorily for a time, until the heavens opened and the rain descended almost solidly for three days. On the third night the sleepers were awakened by the sound of rushing waters. Their floor was afloat, a raft on a sea of mud and rain, and in a few moments the tent made an unsuccessful attempt to act as a sail. Subsequently the use of makeshift floor-boards was strongly discouraged; it was better to sleep in the mud.

It is a relief to turn from these doubtful amusements to the more solid joy of a little horse-racing. It is safe to say that no form of relaxation was more popular amongst the troops.

Considering that we made our own race-courses, with all the appurtenances thereto, the military race meetings were astonishingly successful. There was even a totalisator for those, which meant everybody who could obtain an advance on his pay-book, who liked what is called in racing circles "a flutter"; and there were always several amateur "bookies" as well. The only adjunct familiar to the race-courses at home missing from our meetings was the professional tipster, with his information "straight from the horse's nosebag." As was natural in an army largely composed of cavalry, there were several crack riders well known at home, amongst them at least one who had won the Grand National. This officer, by the way, so the story goes, was turned out of a riding-school one morning because the instructor considered that he did not know how to ride! It would be interesting to know what standard of attainment was required!

Wherever a meeting was held everybody who could beg, borrow, or steal a horse, a mule, or a camel entered it, entirely indifferent of the feelings of the animal in the matter or whether its best distance was five furlongs or five miles.

The camel races, while not exactly regarded as a medium for speculation, were the most amusing to watch. No course was too large for a camel. He zigzagged all over the countryside, and as often as not finished the race with a fine burst into the midst of the spectators. The mules had their moments too; and some of them were nearly as fast as a horse. There was a great deal of speculation, in the literal sense of the word, over the mules; some of them would start, others "dwelt," and others whipped round and made for their stables.

One N.C.O. entered a mule whose chance was esteemed so lightly that the owner-rider was the sole purchaser of a twenty-*piastre* (4s.) ticket at the totalisator. In the race, however, the mule was on his best behaviour and walked away with the prize; his courageous rider received £66 for his faith and his one ticket! This glorious uncertainty was one of the features of military racing and added not a little to the excitement. Army horses, except officers' chargers, are notoriously gregarious by reason of their training, and you could generally be sure of a close finish in any race confined to horses belonging to "other ranks" of the cavalry and artillery.

I believe the infantry on the whole were a great deal worse off in the matter of amusement than were the mounted troops; regimental sports formed the staple joys of their leisure hours, except for boxing matches when they could be arranged; and the latter ran racing very close in the matter of popularity.

When all is said, however, there was singularly little beyond what we made for ourselves which could legitimately be called amusements. The wonder is not that there was actually so little but that there was so much. Our nomadic existence hardly lent itself to the more permanent forms of relaxation. Men occupying a portion of the Jordan Valley one week and the next holding the line on the banks of the river Auja, had neither the time nor the inclination for anything but sleep; we were nearly always on short rations of both water and sleep.

So in the end it came to this: if you wanted a complete change from Palestine you had to go to Egypt for it, either via hospital or on leave. In the latter case, when you had succeeded in the superhuman task of convincing the orderly-room clerk that your name was next on the roster, there came first a long trek across country to railhead. Here you were harassed by an officious person called the R.T.O. who inspected your papers and then scrutinised your person in order to satisfy himself that you were not a criminal escaping from justice. Then you were handed over to an underling who led you to a glorified cattle-truck, whose interior was an amazing jumble of boots, bare knees, helmets, rifles, packs, faces, and drill clothing, and courteously invited you to step inside.

Regardless of the howl of protest from within the truck you thrust a tentative leg over the side, to be met immediately with a muffled but earnest request that you removed your boot from the speaker's face. This little difficulty overcome, perseverance was necessary before you could add your person and kit to the heterogeneous collection already filling the truck. This resolved itself presently into some thirty fellow-sufferers, who, by dint of shuffling and squeezing, made room for yet another on the floor. Then came the thirteen-hour journey to Kantara, followed by another four hours on the Egyptian State Railway to Cairo, or seven to Alexandria. If you accomplished the whole journey without going into hospital you could, on your arrival, consider yourself on leave.

Now in seven days it was impossible to do more than touch the fringe of Cairo. The first three were occupied in accustoming yourself to sleeping in a real bed and to being caged within four walls at night. Then you set yourself to discover interesting places to visit. By the time you had made a selection for the day, it was too late to start for the place and you retired to Groppi's for a *mélange*, with which to console yourself for the disappointment. I knew quite a number of men who neither went to the pyramids, nor saw the Sphinx, nor climbed up to the Citadel to see the mosque of Mahomet Ali, nor penetrated into the bazaars, nor even visited the Zoo. They all said that it took them so long to make up their minds where to go that the day was spent ere they had decided, so they went nowhere. I fancy that a large number of men were so overcome by the unaccustomed sight of shops and streets and people that they did naught but wander round looking at them, breaking off at intervals to eat large and variegated meals. When you think about it this was not a bad way of spending a short leave, especially in a city like Cairo where there was so much to see and so little time to see it in. Moreover, by the time you had settled down to your leave it was over, and you had to face the cattle-trucks once more. All things considered, since home-leave was out of the question, it saved at least a bad attack of nostalgia if you stayed with your comrades up the line and made your own fun.

CHAPTER 18

In the Jordan Valley

The outstanding events of the weeks following the capture of Jerusalem were a brilliant exploit by the 52nd Division on the banks of the River Auja, north of Jaffa, and the establishment of a through connection by rail from Egypt to Jerusalem. The former enterprise was carried out just before Christmas, partly to suppress the Turks who were very active in this region, but chiefly to make the position of our left flank secure. The Turks were very strongly entrenched at Muannis and elsewhere, and between them and the attacking troops, as an additional protection, they had the river, now swollen to many times its usual dimensions by the recent rains, which had also made the ground on either bank little better than a morass. Also, what fords there were had been rendered impassable by the floods, and it was only after prolonged and searching examination, which had always to be undertaken at night and by swimming the river many times, that fairly suitable places were marked out as crossings. One thing only favoured the Scotsmen on the night of the attack: the weather was as tempestuous as could be desired, and the roar of the wind effectually drowned any unavoidable noise and prevented the Turks from receiving intimation of impending trouble. Most of the troops crossed by means of rafts which, after the first one had safely reached the other side, were hauled across by ropes and eventually formed into a rough bridge. Some men, however, actually waded through the raging torrent in water up to the arm-pits, and had the utmost difficulty in getting across safely.

When the division was in position on the other side the attack began at once, in absolute silence, and everywhere the Turks were taken completely by surprise. Practically all the enemy positions were taken at the point of the bayonet, which weapon in the hands of the Scotsmen the enemy disliked exceedingly, and not until shortly after dawn did the firing begin upon those who had not already been killed or captured.

By this excellently stage-managed operation the British line on this part of the front was secured against attack and the important work in connection with the transport could be carried out in safety. The railway was first continued from Gaza to Ludd, after which it swung eastwards to Artuf, where the old Turkish line was utilised as far as Jerusalem; and early in 1918 it was possible to leave Cairo at 6.15 p.m. and be in the Holy City by a quarter to twelve the next morning, the whole journey, with the exception of the ninety-eight miles between Cairo and Kantara, being made on the military railway.

By this fine feat and by their incessant labours on the roads round about Jerusalem the engineers made it possible for an attempt to be made to improve our position on the right. The operations here were of a curiously similar character to those on the left just described, for in each case a swollen and turbulent river loomed large amongst the obstacles to be overcome, and the object—to secure strong flank positions—was in each case the same. But in the second attempt the geographical difficulties alone were enormous. Eastwards from Jerusalem ran what was euphemistically called a road, surely the worst in all Palestine, which led to Jericho and the Jordan valley. From a height of two thousand feet above sea level it descended in a series of jerks, sometimes abruptly, sometimes across a short plateau; it wound round innumerable and execrable corners, it was crossed by *wadis* and streams

191

from all directions, through nearly twenty miles of unimaginable desolation, and finally, after passing the awful travesty that once was Jericho, it reached the river. This road was the main artery in our communications on the right flank.

El Ghor, which comprises the whole of the Jordan Valley, lies thirteen hundred feet below the level of the sea and is without parallel in the universe. Even in March the atmosphere is like that of a Turkish bath and between the river and the mountains of Moab stretches a vast expanse of mud and slippery rocks; a country less suitable for military operations could scarcely be imagined. Thirty miles east of Jericho was the Turkish stronghold Amman, a town on the Hedjaz railway and the objective of the attack, which was undertaken mainly by the 60th (London) Division, the Anzacs, and the Cameliers.

Difficult as had been the crossing of the Auja, that of the Jordan was infinitely worse, for the Turks had destroyed the Ghoraniyeh Bridge; the river was unfordable there by reason of the floods and it was very nearly impossible to cross by swimming elsewhere. Eventually, after many attempts, some men of the 60th Division did succeed in performing the feat, after which rafts were towed across filled with troops who hid in the dense undergrowth lining the banks of the river. It was nearly two days before all the raiding force was safely transported to the other side, for the men as they landed had to beat off the attacks made by the Turks to prevent the crossing and they were under heavy fire all the time. On March 24th, when the enemy had been cleared out of the high ground near the Jordan, the London division started off through the mud to attack the pass of Shunet Nimrin, which commanded the road to Es Salt, a town in the mountains of Moab and the first objective in the assault on Amman, a dozen miles beyond. The cavalry struck across country farther to the south, making for an important section of the Hedjaz railway which they hoped to blow up before the Turks could rally in its defence. It was fortunate that the delay in crossing the Jordan had been no greater; as it was, the 60th Division had incalculable trouble in storming Shunet Nimrin, though their difficulties came not so much from the opposition, desperately as the Turks fought, as from the nature of the country leading to the pass, which virtually precluded the use of artillery in support and forced the infantry to bear the whole burden of the attack.

Now struggling through the heavy mud, now scrambling over the rocks, in places so steep that the men had to climb on to each other's shoulders in order to proceed, the Londoners rushed the Turkish positions, and following up their success hustled the enemy to such purpose that Es Salt was captured practically without opposition. But the advance did not stop here, for every moment was of value, and though they had now been marching and fighting for four days in unspeakable conditions, the infantry began their twenty-mile march to Amman. The road was utterly impossible for wheeled traffic, and, in the pitiless downpour, next to impossible for the infantry, bowed down by the weight of saturated packs and clothing, whose boots were clogged with mud and hampered the already dragging feet. It was three days before the Amman plain was reached! The cavalry and the "Cameliers," advancing from the south, were obliged to travel over tracks which would have given a mountain goat the horrors, across *wadis* and *nullahs* so steep that the horses had to be let down by ropes and hauled up the other side, while the Cameliers had to build their roads as they went along, a camel being rather an inconvenient beast on which to scale the slippery sides of a cliff. So, slithering, scrambling, and fighting all the way, they came at last to Amman, like the infantry, almost too spent for further exertions. With never a pause for rest, however, the combined forces on March 28th made an attack on the Turkish positions, having little artillery support—two batteries of R.H.A. had, I think, succeeded in getting their guns through the mud—and already weakened by their terrible privations.

For three days the battle raged, wave after wave of infantry staggering forward undaunted, hardly knowing their direction except that it was towards the enemy, while the cavalry made repeated efforts to storm the great hill defending the town and the Cameliers operated in the centre. But the odds were too great: not only did the Turks possess all the advantage of ground, for their positions could only be approached across a plain swept from end to end by rifle, machine-gun and artillery fire, but from the Judean hills reinforcements poured into Amman to aid in its defence and to cut off if possible the whole of the raiding force.

It was this latter contingency as well as the utter futility of persevering in the assault, that made a retirement imperative, and on the third night of the battle the exhausted men began their march back to the Jordan, picking up on their way the garrisons left at Shunet Nimrin and Es Salt, together with some hundreds of prisoners. A large proportion of the Christian inhabitants of the latter place who feared, with good reason, ill-treatment by the Turks, also joined the column with such meagre belongings as they could hurriedly snatch together. This influx of extra mouths to feed strained the already overburdened resources to the utmost, but the refugees were well looked after both on the retreat and afterwards in Jerusalem, and most of the children were brought along by the mounted troops so that they should not suffer undue fatigue.

It is but piling on the agony to dwell upon the details of the retreat to the Jordan; it is sufficient to say that it seemed to be the concentrated essence of all that had gone before, and that on the eleventh day after the commencement of the raid the crossing was again safely accomplished. Although it was unsuccessful, I suggest that as a triumph over privation and fatigue, and for extreme gallantry under most trying conditions of battle, the venture is without parallel in British military history, especially in regard to the infantry, who had marched and fought almost continuously for ten days. The mounted

In the Jordan Valley—Wadi Auja

troops would, I think, be the first to grant them pride of place, for, as I have tried to show elsewhere, whatever happened, we counted ourselves fortunate who had a horse or a camel to ride in Palestine. Poor brutes! Those who returned from the raid on Amman were in a pitiable plight. Some of the camels had not had their heavy saddles off for eight days, and when at last they were removed the flesh of the flanks and back came away with them.

The net result of this affair was the formation of a bridge-head at Ghoraniyeh, which during the first fortnight in April the Turks made strong attempts to retake, without success; and they finally contented themselves with fortifying the pass of Shunet Nimrin and placing a powerful garrison there in order to frustrate any further raids on Amman.

With the end of the rains and the rapid approach of summer came a period of sheer torment for our troops in the Jordan Valley. The mud changed to a fine, powdery dust, which rose in clouds at the slightest movement, myriads of flies awoke from their long winter sleep, and clouds of mosquitoes arrived for their annual feast. Drill shorts, which formerly had been the general summer wear, were now strictly forbidden to the mounted troops, who were forced to endure the sticky agony of riding-breeches every hour of the twenty-four in order to expose as little as possible of their persons to the unremitting attacks of these pestilential insects. Also, the bivouac areas were infested with small but poisonous snakes who had, like scorpions, a fondness for army blankets; and it is no exaggeration to say that a man went to sleep every night with the full consciousness that he might never wake again. Finally, as if these inflictions were not enough, droves of Turkish aeroplanes came over daily and scientifically bombed all the camps in the valley. The camels in particular made an excellent mark and suffered severely, though apart from this, they were the only living creatures appertaining to the army who flourished and waxed fat in that blistering lime-kiln.

Towards the end of April a heavy concentration of cavalry round Jericho made it evident that another attempt was to be made east of the Jordan, and on the night of the 28th-29th the 1st Australian Mounted Division crossed the river and advanced due north, between the east bank and the foothills, towards the Turkish road from Nablus to Es Salt and the ford known as Jisr ed Damieh, whence they were to march east for the purpose of cutting off the retreat of the garrison at Shunet Nimrin should the attack of the 60th Division on that place prevail. Soon after dawn the cavalry came under very heavy fire, but pushed forward and attained their objectives, where two brigades, without artillery, went off to help the Londoners. The latter marched all night, and, taking the Turks by surprise in the early hours, stormed part of the pass, but despite all their efforts could make no further headway.

Meanwhile the 4th Light Horse and a brigade of horse-artillery were heavily engaged till dusk in holding off reinforcements from Nablus who were attempting to cross by the Jisr ed Damieh ford. After nightfall this brigade and the batteries retired a short distance and took up a position commanding the road, in a deep *wadi* where the guns had to be man-handled into place, after which the wagons and limbers were let down the sides of the *wadi* by means of drag-ropes, and the horses scrambled down as best they could. Dawn brought the news that the Turks had successfully crossed the Jordan during the night, and had followed the river southwards in the direction of our second bridgehead at El Auja, intending to come at the left flank of the Light Horse, which was absolutely in the air.

At seven o'clock they attacked, and plastered the batteries in the *wadi* with shells till, at the end of two hours, the position became untenable, and an attempt was made to shift the guns. It was incomparably more difficult to get out of the *wadi* than it had been to get in, and moving was but out of the frying-pan into the fire, for one *wadi* led into another, and the sides were so precipitous that the horses were almost useless for dragging out the guns. Four teams were hooked into a gun, but the ground made it impossible for more than half a dozen horses at a time to be in draught, and when at last the position was cleared the horses slithered down the sides of the *wadis*, and guns and wagons overturned at the bottom in hopeless and inextricable confusion.

Frantically the gunners strove to get them out, some harnessing themselves to the drag-ropes and others shoving on the wheels; but every effort was to no purpose, and meanwhile horses and men were being shot down on all hands by the advancing Turks, whose cries of "Allah! Allah!" could now be plainly heard. At last the inevitable order was given to clear out with such horses as remained, for it was impossible to move, much less save the guns, and after these had been rendered useless to the enemy, the gallant gunners reluctantly withdrew.

The moment they were clear of the foothills they galloped into an inferno of machine-gun fire at close quarters from the Germans and Turks occupying *wadis* and shell-holes all over the plain. Horses were shot down right and left, and a team of eight which had not been unhooked were all hit, together with two of the drivers, who fortunately managed to get safely away. Finally the shattered remnants of the artillery brigade assembled at Ghoraniyeh bridgehead, while the Light Horse fell back towards Es Salt, which the other two brigades had succeeded in occupying. By their clever manoeuvring, however, the Turks had rendered the position both of the Australians in Es Salt and the 60th Division in front of Nimrin so precarious that another withdrawal was urgently necessary, and after the Londoners had made a last desperate attempt to storm the pass, the retirement was carried out successfully and without loss, though in bitter disappointment at a second failure; that it was the only time in the whole campaign when British guns were captured by the Turks was remarkably poor consolation.

CHAPTER 19

The Valley of Chaos

During the summer of 1918 great changes took place in
the personnel of the army in Palestine. The early success of
the great German offensive in France had caused the "S.O.S."
to be sent out for other and more men to stem the tide of advance, and all the other British fronts were denuded of white
troops, in whose place, so far as Palestine was concerned, came
Indians, many of whom had only a few months' service to
their credit. The infantry of the 52nd Lowland Division, who
apparently had not done sufficient fighting for one War, left
to give a hand to their comrades in France, as did the 74th,
still acting as infantry, and all the remaining divisions sent at
least one brigade; large numbers of cavalry and artillery also
went overseas. Practically all the summer, therefore, was devoted to re-organising the forces and training the levies from
India. The principle adopted in the infantry was to brigade
one British battalion to every three Indian battalions right
through the divisions; and this acted very well indeed, for the
white troops provided just that leaven of steadiness lacking
in the young Indians. In the cavalry much the same principle was adopted, but the artillery first tried the experiment
of employing Egyptians as drivers in the ammunition-wagon
teams, retaining the British drivers for the guns.

For a time all went well with the training of these Egyptians, until, as a test of their efficiency, night operations were

ordered, which included a dash into a *wadi* and out the other side. This effort produced what can only be described as a *shemozzle*: horses, wagons, and men piled themselves up in a hopeless tangle at the bottom of the *wadi*, and the night operations came to an abrupt end. In the searching inquiry which followed it was discovered by the medical authorities that less than twenty-five per cent. of these Egyptians could see clearly at night, a further twenty-five per cent. were stone-blind after sunset, and of the remainder, the most that could be said was that they could just see in the dark and that was all! When the weeding-out process was completed the British personnel returned as lead-drivers; Indians were added to make up the numbers, and this curious mixture acted satisfactorily.

A remarkable feature of the spring and summer was the gradual rise to power of the Royal Air Force, culminating in complete supremacy over the Turks immediately before and during the autumn campaign. Presumably a ship had at last arrived with adequate machines, for all through the summer long-distance bombing raids were undertaken with conspicuous success; and for the first time our planes "had the wings" of the Turks. One great raid was carried out after a report had been received that three German divisions were on their way south from Constantinople to reinforce the Turk. The trains containing two of the divisions were almost completely destroyed before they reached Damascus; the third division arrived more or less intact, and went into action in the Jordan Valley, where they were so badly mauled by the Australians that the fragments that remained bolted incontinently, and for the future stayed behind the line. In August the R.A.F., in conjunction with the forces of the King of the Hedjaz, who were working their way northwards across the desert east of Amman, made an attack on the Hedjaz railway at Der'aa, at which place the line was completely demolished and all communication severed with the north.

In single combats, too, our airmen now more than held their own, for the Turkish planes either fled at first sight or, if they stayed to argue the point, were generally brought down. From the Camel Camp on the hill overlooking General Allenby's Headquarters at Bir Salem we saw several battles in the air, for G.H.Q. was a favourite mark of the Turks, and these almost invariably went in favour of the British.

By the end of August the intensive training of the new troops and the work of re-organisation were complete; and it is interesting to note, as an indication of the way in which the army had been for the most part, made "on the premises," as it were, that it comprised British, French, Italian, Jewish, West Indian, Arab, Indian, Algerian, Armenian, and Egyptian troops, to say nothing of the tribes of mixed race but Mohammedan faith who assisted the King of the Hedjaz in the final struggle.

At this stage a word as to the disposition of the Turkish forces is necessary: their main position was at Nablus, (the ancient Shechem), which was well protected naturally by Mt. Gerizim in the south and Mt. Ebal in the north, and had been fortified with German thoroughness and ingenuity during the summer months. From here the line extended in a south-westerly direction towards the sea, including en route another immensely strong position at Jiljulieh, immediately to the north of which was the village of Kalkilieh, also well fortified; another Turkish force operated west and east of the Jordan.

A frontal attack on Nablus was out of the question; an army of goats might have successfully scaled the mountains of Samaria, but it was no place for troops; nor was the Jordan Valley any more inviting. The best chance of success lay in the coastal sector, where the conformation of the ground was not so much in favour of the Turks, and it was decided that our main attack should be made here. The plan was for the infantry to make a wide breach in the Turkish line by storming the defences between Jiljulieh and the sea, whereupon the cavalry were to sweep forward on to the Esdraelon Plain and close all possible lines of retreat to the Turks, while at the same time an outflanking movement was to be carried out by the troops in the eastern sector.

The main difficulties were to concentrate unseen a large force of infantry in the plain of Sharon, and to bring the remainder of the cavalry from the Jordan Valley without observation by the enemy. The vast olive-groves round about Ludd and Jaffa comfortably concealed the infantry, whose movements were carried out at night and with the utmost caution, but the transport of the cavalry was a tougher problem, for the Turks were very much on the alert in the Jordan Valley, and did in fact expect the attack to be made in this direction.

Considerable guile was therefore necessary, into which entered a little innocent fun. It was a general and strictly enforced rule that no lights should be shown after dusk, on account of bombing raids, yet during the last weeks of August long lines of bivouac fires twinkled nightly in the Jordan Valley; and the authorities seemed to be singularly blind to this flagrant disobedience of orders. During the day at stated hours groups of men riding aged and infirm horses were strung out at 50-yard intervals, engaged in the gentle pastime of dragging sacks and branches along the roads; they made so much dust that it might easily have been caused by, say, a cavalry division going to water. Also, thousands of tiny tents sprang up round the bivouac areas, in front of which were equally diminutive soldiers in squads and companies, whose function it was to stand rigidly to attention all day long, and who treated the frequent bombing raids with utter contempt. A careful observer would have noticed a certain woodenness about them, but enemy airmen were profoundly impressed by this large concentration of troops.

Meanwhile every night brigade after brigade of British cavalry left the Jordan Valley on their fifty-mile ride across country to the friendly shelter of the orange-groves of Jaffa and Sarona, and the men left behind complained bitterly of the increase of work in having to light so many extra bivouac fires! The whole concentration was carried out without the Turks being any the wiser, and by the middle of September thirty-five thousand infantry were ready to pour forth from their hiding-places, with four divisions of mounted troops to follow hard upon their heels; it was scarcely possible to move in the coast sector without falling over a battery of artillery, and tucked away round Richon and Duran were thousands of transport camels of every shade and breed.

At dusk on the night of September 18th the orange-groves began to erupt, and for eight hours horse and foot in orderly columns marched silently forward, the infantry to their bat-tle positions and the cavalry to the beach between Arsuf and Jaffa, there to wait till the breach had been made. At half-past four the next morning the shattering roar of artillery proclaimed that the offensive had begun, and at dawn the infantry attacked the Turkish positions, swept over those near-est the coast at the first onslaught, and then swung eastwards. One after another from Et Tireh to Jiljulieh, strongholds upon which months of labour had been expended fell before the irresistible élan of our men, though the Turks fought magnifi-cently to hold their line. By noon the whole of the coastal sector was in our hands, and the plain of Sharon lay open to the cavalry, who had started on their historic ride north soon after our first attack.

In the meantime the infantry, driving before them the demoralised remnants of the Turkish 8th Army, captured Tul Keram, Turkish G.H.Q., together with a host of prisoners, and then continued east to help the Welsh and Irish divisions in their assault on Nablus. The Turks here had no information of the debacle on their right, for the R.A.F. had started out at dawn and had destroyed every means of communication, except the roads, between the two armies. They therefore fought with the utmost determination, and aided by their well-chosen and well-fortified positions, held off our attacks all that day and the next, though the Irishmen by extraordinary exertions crumpled up one flank. Then the last message ever sent from the north informed them that the British cavalry had overrun the whole country in their rear, so far as they knew the only line of retreat left open to them was eastward across the Jordan, and this loophole, too, was soon to be closed. Panic reigned; the roads leading east were black with long columns of guns and transport and men mingled in hopeless confusion, fleeing with no thought of anything but their own safety; a routed, utterly demoralised rabble.

Nablus was occupied without difficulty on the 21st, but the infantry, who had been scrambling about the hills of Samaria for three days, could not run fast enough to catch the Turks, who were making their way through the Wadi Farah towards the Jisr ed Damieh ford. Half-way through the *wadi* the road has on one side a deep, gloomy gorge, while on the other stretch gaunt hills terrible in their desolation and stony barrenness. The whole aspect of the place is sinister and forbidding in the extreme, and one can imagine the panic-stricken Turks hurrying through yet a little faster, eager to sight the yellow waters of the Jordan. But they never reached the goal, for the Royal Air Force found the column half-way through the gorge. Relays of machines joined in the attack, first dropping bombs and then flying low and spraying the column with bullets. In five minutes the road eastwards was blocked, and driven by the slow but remorseless advance of our infantry far in the rear, with impassable hills on the one hand, and a precipice on the other, the column was caught in a trap.

A part of it tried to escape, before being driven into the gorge, by a road leading to the north, but were bombed back again into the shambles. Mad with terror, some of the Turks tried to scramble up the steep hills, others made an attempt to descend into the deep gorge; anywhere to escape from the awful hail of bombs and bullets. For four hours the slaughter continued, and when "Cease fire" was ordered, the road for nine miles was literally a vast charnel-house. Guns, limbers, commissariat-wagons, field-kitchens, every conceivable form of vehicle, including a private barouche, lay heaped together in monstrous confusion; and when night fell ragged, half-starved Bedouins descended upon the stricken valley, stealing from pile to pile of debris in search of loot, nor could the rifles of the guards deter them from the ghoulish task. It took an entire division three weeks to clear the roads and bury the dead.

Isolated columns from the Turkish 7th Army did succeed in reaching the Jordan, but were all killed or captured by the mounted troops left in the valley. Daily the toll of prisoners increased, as hundreds of Turks who had been in hiding in the hills round Samaria and Nablus were driven by hunger to give themselves up to the searching parties. Ras el Ain, which had been a part of our front line, presented an extraordinary spectacle, for most of the prisoners passed through here on their way south to Wilhelma and beyond. For thirty-six hours there was hardly a break in the procession shambling towards the great hill on which stand the ruins of Herod's Castle, where Salome danced for the head of John the Baptist, and where now the prisoners were caged. There was a marked difference between the condition of the Turkish prisoners and that of the Germans: the former were ragged, half-starved, and yellow with privation and fatigue, but all the Germans I saw were sleek, well-clad, and bearing every sign of good living. It was impossible to cage them together, for they fought like cats with each other on every possible occasion, and caused endless trouble to the guards, who had to go amongst them with the bayonet in order to separate them.

Meanwhile, what of the cavalry whose business it had been to cut the Turkish lines of communication with Damascus and the north? Their chief objectives were El Afule,

A WATER CONVOY

THE VALLEY OF CHAOS—BEFORE THE TURKISH RETREAT

which might briefly be described as a place where all roads meet, Nazareth, a few miles farther north, the headquarters of the German General, Liman von Sanders, the Commander-in-Chief of the Turks, and Jenin, the headquarters of the enemy Air Force. They met with practically no opposition until they reached the entrance to the Esdraelon Plain, which is approached through a narrow pass, where a weak garrison was easily overwhelmed and captured. Had the Turks had time to fortify this pass it is possible that the whole course of events might have been changed, for it commanded the way to the main arteries in the Turkish communications, upon the capture of which everything depended. But the surprise was complete; the fine work of the British airmen had prevented news of the destruction of the front line from reaching enemy headquarters, and their first intimation of our success was the sight of the cavalry streaming over the Esdraelon Plain towards Afule.

Most of the small garrisons on the way were literally taken in their beds, and when the few stragglers who escaped brought the tidings to Afule it was too late to make any great show of resistance. Thousands of Turks surrendered here, without attempting to fight, and when the Germans also had been roped in, the number of prisoners far exceeded that of the attacking cavalry. The loot was prodigious, for Afule was one of the main depots of the enemy, and every house occupied by Germans showed signs of the extreme solicitude they had for their personal comfort; that of the Turks did not matter. In the hill upon which the town stands were numerous caves filled to overflowing with choice wines, cognac, tobacco and delicacies which made the mouths of the beholders, who had had neither bite nor sup for thirty-six hours, water in anticipation. An Australian trooper told me afterwards that there was sufficient wine in Afule and Nazareth for every man in the Expeditionary Force, at a bottle per head, and added naïvely that he had had his bottle just at the time it was most needed!

The column advancing on Nazareth had met with equal though not quite bloodless success. Arriving at dawn they, too, found the town asleep, and clattered through the streets in search of Liman von Sanders. He was warned in the very nick of time, however, and the cavalry had an interesting back view of a swiftly disappearing car in which sat Liman von Sanders in his pyjamas, followed at a respectful distance by some of his staff not so discreetly clad. Undisturbed by the defection of their Chief, the Germans resisted stoutly for a time, both in the streets of Nazareth and in the hills north of the town, but ultimately all were gathered in and sent across the ancient battlefield of Armageddon to join the rest at Afule.

The aerodromes at Jenin were captured, or, to be more exact, rendered useless by our aircraft, who had hovered over them ever since the beginning of the battle, dropping an "egg" whenever enemy machines attempted to come out. When the cavalry arrived, practically all they had to do was to tie up the hordes of men who were only too anxious to surrender.

In five days the combined forces had smashed up two Turkish armies and had taken forty thousand prisoners. I cannot do better than end this chapter by giving in full General Allenby's letter to the troops thanking them for this remarkable achievement: "I desire to convey to all ranks and all arms of the Force under my command, my admiration and thanks for the great deeds of the past week, and my appreciation of their gallantry and determination, which have resulted in the total destruction of the 7th and 8th Turkish Armies opposed to us. Such a complete victory has seldom been known in all the history of war."

CHAPTER 20

In Full Cry

At this stage the campaign developed into a species of fox-hunt on an enormous scale, with the Turk very adequately playing the part of the fox. Although some forty thousand of the enemy had been captured in the grand attack, a similar number still remained at large who were running very hard in the direction of Beyrout and Damascus, and these it was our business to pursue. Also, the King of the Hedjaz emerged from the desert east of Amman, and in conjunction with the Australians, fell upon the 4th Turkish Army, who were still making some show of resistance in the mountains of Moab, captured most of them, and started the remainder on the long road to Damascus.

Thus the hunt was up on both flanks, the infantry for the most part following the coast route and the Hedjaz column riding via Der'aa.

In the centre, with a long start, the cavalry who had poured through the first gap in the Turkish line were still riding hard after the enemy. The cavalry travelled so quickly that they missed, I think, much of the interest of the journey, which took them through the centre of a country wherein almost every village has a history; the reader, therefore, will perhaps find the slower gait of the Camels more to his taste.

The prisoners were still pouring in when we left Ras el Ain, and in the eyes of those we passed was an awful glassy stare as of men who had come through great torment: these were they who had come out of the Valley of Chaos alive.

Here and there a German officer walked alone at the head of a batch of Turks, and as this was a sufficiently unusual sight, I asked one of the guards the reason. He replied that many of the Turkish battalions were commanded by German officers, whose principal asset was a firm belief in discipline as practised in the Fatherland. Hated and feared by Turkish officers, and contemptuously regarded as inferiors by officers of their own blood, in captivity neither party would own them: they were Ishmaelites.

The attitude of our camel drivers towards the Turks was somewhat amusing, though it is to be feared that pity is a quality but little understood by Eastern nations. "Turkey finish!" they would say with an indescribable shrug of the shoulders, and this expression, about the only English they knew, seemed to afford them infinite satisfaction.

In the early stages our route lay across the recent battlefield, where on every hand were the terrible signs of a routed army: dead horses, the wreckage of guns and wagons, rifles with the murderous saw-bayonet attached—a monstrous weapon for any nation to use, little clusters of shells near dismantled battery positions, long rows of sharpened stakes in front of a trench smashed almost out of recognition, and endless barbed-wire torn and blown into grotesque piles by the violence of our bombardment; and through the debris slunk the predatory Bedouin with his dingy *galabeah* full of loot. At one place a Turkish camel with a gaily caparisoned saddle trotted up to us and joined the column for company; he earned his keep, too, after he had recovered from the effects of his long fast and had been fattened up again. While on the subject of animals let me state that on this first day a goat, an ass, another camel, and numerous pariah dogs added themselves to our ration strength.

The goat earned opprobrium and early demise by eat-ing one of my notebooks, which contained a nominal roll of some two hundred camel-drivers; and as each native has at least four names—Abdul Achmed Mohammed Khalil is a fair example—the fact that we made several meals off the goat was not adequate compensation for the labour of re-writing the roll. The ass performed the duty to which he has been accustomed from time immemorial in the Holy Land: he carried the aged. In the company we had a number of old men who had joined the corps probably because they had sons already serving, and we used to allow the old fellows to ride in turn upon the ass, particularly towards the end of a long day's march. The number of these "Abu's" (fathers) who developed a pronounced limp at some time or other during the day was astonishing, but the sudden and miraculous cure that was effected by the appearance of the Bash-Rais (native Sergeant-Major) completely bewildered the uninitiated. The second camel, being too young to carry a load, was killed, and gave me my first taste of camel-steak, which in flavour is not unlike veal.

Of the pariah dogs I dare not trust myself to say much. They would follow the convoy all day long, with the furtive air characteristic of those to whom life means nothing but a constant dodging of half-bricks violently hurled; and at night they would sit around in a circle and perform the mournful operation known as baying the moon, which they did with prodigious enthusiasm and complete indifference as to whether there was a moon or not. It will convey much when I add that there was a deplorable lack of suitable stones along the roadside.

After leaving Tul Keram, a hill town whose white mosque was a landmark for miles, we turned westwards and struck across the plain of Sharon towards the sea. Hereabouts the country with its red soil and glorious verdure is not unlike some parts of Somerset in appearance. The harvest had been gathered in, and we passed through vast fields of stubble, which were divided one from another by strips of curious coloured grass. Indeed, this bluish grass and the cactus-hedges were the only forms of boundary used in Palestine and Syria; I never saw a wall except one built by the troops for defensive purposes.

At one part of the trek the road led through a tunnel, very nearly half a mile in length, which was formed by a double row of vines whose branches bent over a kind of trellis-work; and on either side of this leafy tunnel were orchards of pomegranate and fig-trees. Dessert was plentiful for some days. There was little evidence now of the destructive hand of war, except that no one was working in the orchards and vineries, and the inhabitants of the small native villages through which we passed mostly remained behind closed doors, with not even an inquisitive eye at the window.

Caesarea seemed quite busy by contrast, when we arrived in the cool of evening, though it is only a tiny fishing-village whose tumbledown mud-huts are completely overshadowed by the great masses of ruins with which the rocks are covered. As with other ruined sites in this country of ruins, it was difficult to realise that Caesarea once represented the might of Rome, as an imperial city and the most considerable port in Palestine. Jaffa must have been small and mean by comparison, for Herod the Great not only built after the pattern of Rome a great city of pillars and columns, but constructed an artificial harbour deep enough to float any ship of his time; nor were the defences neglected, for the city was once in its history besieged for seven years! Of the harbour nothing now remains, and, to come back to the present, the water was scarcely deep enough to float the lighters of the merchant-ships landing rations for the division.

We had the Mediterranean for company after leaving Caesarea, except for an occasional brief incursion inland where the coast was too dangerous for traffic. On one of these detours we passed through Zimmerin, a German colony magnificently situated on a hillside and surrounded by a great forest. Here in times of peace lumbering was carried on, though whether the Germans followed Solomon's example, and floated rafts of timber down to Jaffa or north to Haifa, I was unable to ascertain. At any rate there seemed to be no other way to get their timber to the markets.

I wonder how many people are aware of the extent to which the Germans carried their policy of "peaceful penetration" in Palestine and Syria? Whenever in our wanderings we came across a neat, modern town or village, be sure that the inhabitants were mainly German; that in many cities they were also Jews does not, I suggest, make a great deal of difference.

The language of all was German, and their extraordinary thoroughness in devising means to overcome the climatic and other difficulties of the country was also German, with the result that they waxed fat and prosperous, while the people indigenous to the soil scraped a precarious living by tending the flocks and tilling the land of the interlopers. All through the country from Gaza, where there was actually a German school, to Haifa, of which the largest and wealthiest portion of the population was German, you will find these colonies occupying almost invariably the most commanding sites and situated in the midst of the most fertile tracts of land.

It was, I think, by contrast with these prosperous places that the ruins of Palestine and Syria took on an added desolation and loneliness: you could with difficulty visualise the past splendours of a crumbling mass of mighty pillars when on the hill opposite stood a town of bijou villas with modern appurtenances.

A mournful example of this was at Athlit, the remains of whose greatness lay half-buried almost at the foot of Mt. Carmel. For a brief moment you could capture the spirit of a bygone age; the massive walls seemed to ring again with the clash of arms and the shouts of that little band of Crusaders who were fighting their last fight in their last stronghold on holy soil. Then your eyes lit on the great barrack of a German hotel on the top of Carmel, and the great fortress dissolved into a crumbling, shapeless pile at your feet. Beyond Athlit lay the port of Haifa, a town of considerable size, which contained the largest German colony in the country. The road leading into and out of Haifa is typical of the Eastern mind; that is, it is anything but straight.

After you have left what might be called the west-end of the town, which is inhabited by the Germans, the road winds interminably through the native quarter apparently undecided what to do. Eventually it turns and climbs the lower slopes of Mt. Carmel until, very nearly at the top, for no reason whatever that I could see, it makes up its mind to descend again. After about four hours of meandering you find yourself on the outskirts of the town, wiping a heated brow and wondering aggrievedly why the wretched road could not do its business properly.

Seen from the vicinity of the "brook Kishon," where we camped that night, Haifa is a beautifully clean-looking town of modern stone houses each with its little cluster of trees round it, built on the mountain-side high above the malaria-infested flats which stretch eastwards towards the Esdraelon Plain. The inhabitants seemed uncommonly glad to see British troops, and gave the sailors who were granted shore-leave a particularly warm welcome. It was pleasant to hear some news, after being "off the map" for five days. The cavalry had been doing amazing things, for they started from Nazareth almost immediately after its capture and rode westwards to Haifa, which they stormed in face of strong opposition. Another party rode on to Acre, twelve miles away, capturing it without difficulty; after which the two forces joined up and turned east again towards the Sea of Galilee. Meanwhile the cavalry coming from the Jordan Valley had been fighting constantly with the stray bodies of Turks encountered on the northward march.

Resistance was for the most part unorganised; but at Semakh, a town at the southern end of the Sea of Galilee, the Turks made a most determined effort to save the railway. The Australians, however, were in a hurry; they wanted to be the first troops to reach Damascus, and would brook no delay. Semakh was taken by a brilliant and impetuous charge which carried the Australians through the defences and ended in the Sea of Galilee, as also did large numbers of the enemy!

Royal Tiberias was occupied next, after which both the eastern and western forces started on the hundred-mile ride to Damascus, which necessitated a climb from six hundred feet below sea level to nearly three thousand above. Again there was some desultory but bitter fighting, notably at the Jordan soon after the march had begun, but the cavalry carried everything before them, and, riding day and night, reached Damascus on October 1st, after a final burst of thirty-six hours in the saddle. In the ten days since the opening of the offensive they had covered upwards of two hundred and fifty miles, a feat which for endurance alone on the part of men and horses has not been equalled in this War.

In that time they had cleared the greater part of Syria of the enemy, and had captured or driven into the hands of the more slowly advancing infantry over eighty thousand prisoners, with practically all the guns and transport in the Turkish Army. Virtually the fighting was over, since almost the entire enemy force had been accounted for, the few thousands still at large being a disorganised rabble, incapable of further resistance.

But news of a greater peril than War reached Haifa. Famine stalked naked through the land of Lebanon; and it was urgently necessary to send help to the starving inhabitants of Beyrout and the surrounding country. Political reasons, too, demanded that we should occupy as much territory as possible. On October 3rd, therefore, we marched out of Haifa and began the long journey north.

CHAPTER 21

Over the Ladder of Tyre

Behold us, then, once more on the high road—or, to be more accurate, the broad firm sands leading to Acre. We were all mighty pleased to be on the move again, partly because Haifa was not a deliriously exciting place to be in, but chiefly because the neighbourhood of the famous river Kishon was singularly uninviting, and when the rains came, would be a veritable plague-spot of malaria and blackwater fever.

We did not need the history books to tell us that Acre was, and is, a fortress; for the great battlements are still standing, and the massive walls show little signs of decay. Magnificently situated on a promontory at the northern end of the bay, it rears its head proudly, as becomes a city that in twelve hundred years has withstood more sieges than almost any city in Palestine. It is, too, essentially English in its associations: from the time of the Crusaders, whose chief stronghold it was, down to within hailing distance of our own day.

Except for an itinerant stone-merchant the country around has few attractions; and as we proceeded it grew rougher and more difficult to negotiate, until it reached a point where all progress seemed likely to come to an abrupt end. A huge spur of rock, jutting far out into the sea and shutting off the beach, completely blocked the way; it was as though we had come to the limits of one country with this great sentinel to bar our entrance into another. It was the Ladder of Tyre, the geographical barrier between Palestine and the Land of Canaan; and we had to climb over it somehow.

Having negotiated a small hill in the foreground we descended into a steep gully with innumerable twists and turns, ever growing more difficult and dangerous. As the place was strewn with boulders the camels had great trouble in finding a foothold, particularly with the additional handicap of two bales of *tibben* or sacks of grain, which oscillated dangerously with the uneven movement. Presently the slope became more gradual, though not less rough in surface, and finally the path began to ascend towards the Ladder itself. Cut in the face of the rock were broad but shallow steps, in some places worn almost flat by the passage of countless thousands of feet. Indian pioneers were hard at work on the Ladder and had already, in the short time at their disposal, done wonders in the way of removing the litter of stones that covered the steps, blasting away portions of overhanging rock, and building rough ramparts on the side nearest the sea. The camels approached it very gingerly at first, but after one or two had "refused," tackled the climb. About half-way up the cliff there was a sort of platform which marked the turn in the Ladder; here a false step meant destruction, for it was a sheer drop down to the sea three hundred feet below.

A pioneer chose the precise moment at which I reached this platform to touch off a small blasting charge, the noise of which so startled my mare that she very nearly stepped off the edge; and a piece of rock hit a camel and all but started a stampede. After that, being a person of small courage, I dismounted and walked.

The descent was even worse than the ascent for the camels, for the steps were not only broad but wide from back to front, and it needed a big stride successfully to negotiate them. I found it difficult enough on foot; how the camels accomplished it without mishap, carrying their heavy burdens, will ever remain a mystery.

Eventually we reached the level ground on the other side, and continued along the shore as far as Tyre, a town nowadays of poverty-stricken fishermen, with scarcely anything visible of the ancient city. *"I will make thee a terror, and thou shalt be no more: though thou be sought for, yet shalt thou never be found again, saith the Lord God";* thus spoke Ezekiel the Prophet concerning the fate of Tyre, and his words are literally true to-day.

We began shortly to come upon the real beauties of the Land of Canaan. The road was bordered in many places by fruit trees of all kinds, overhanging so far that you had only to reach out your hand to pick the fruit as you rode along. Also, there were numerous orchards and kitchen-gardens with whose owners we used to bargain for the produce. Curiously enough we had extraordinary difficulty in persuading the people to take Egyptian money: they would insist on having Turkish money in spite of our reiterated assertions that it had suffered a serious slump in value. One old lady to whom I showed a Turkish one pound note—worth about the cost of printing—simply jumped at it, and immediately fished out an enormous bag of small change. She was quite upset at my refusal to part with the note; and we haggled for a quarter of an hour about whether she would give me, roughly, sixteen shillings-worth of Turkish silver for a piece of worthless paper, or whether she would accept five *piastres* Egyptian in exchange for a hatful of limes.

The camel-drivers thoroughly enjoyed this part of the trek; indeed, they were in amazingly high spirits the whole way, despite the long daily march. They had as much water as they could drink, a great thing for the Egyptian native, there was fruit for the picking on the trees, and everything was free! So they imagined, but the exasperated ladies who were continually coming to complain that a sportsman in a blue *galabeah* was rifling their orchards evidently thought otherwise.

All the camel-men had the predatory instinct strongly developed, and they were adepts at concealing the "evidence,"

THE VALLEY OF CHAOS—AFTER THE BOMBING RAID

which sometimes was very much more than fruit or eggs. On one occasion the convoy passed an old man driving a flock of sheep, of which one mysteriously disappeared. I happened to be riding immediately behind the flock and saw nothing unusual, yet some time after the old man caught us up at the midday halt and complained that one of the camel-men had stolen a sheep. We searched the convoy from end to end and found no trace; we even went so far as to search the men's clothing! and ultimately the old man had to go away without his sheep.

Curiously enough, a leg of mutton appeared in the mess that night; and a very welcome change it was, too, from bully-beef.

I can offer no explanation of the phenomenon; I only know that we searched the convoy conscientiously and thoroughly and there was no sign of mutton, dead or alive. It must have needed marvellous sleight-of-hand to conceal a full-grown sheep from view!

That was the reverse side of the medal: the obverse was much brighter. It was impossible not to admire the extraordinary endurance of the camel-men. They would march fifteen to twenty miles a day for days, and even weeks at a time, provided only that they had enough water; and, well led, they would go anywhere and do anything.

On the fifth day out from Haifa we marched into Sidon, whose inhabitants turned out en masse and welcomed the column with great and spontaneous enthusiasm, which left no doubt as to its genuineness, though at times it became a trifle embarrassing. On the surface the people looked little the worse for four years' privations and ill-treatment at the hands of the Turks, but a glance into the shops as we passed showed little else but fruit in the shape of food; and this is not very satisfying as a sole diet. In some parts of the town pinched faces and wan cheeks were frequent; and one group consisting of an elderly man with his wife and two daughters especially attracted my attention. Their faces were dead-white, as if they had been living below ground for years, and the dull, stunned look of misery in their eyes was terrible to see; obviously they had not yet fully realised their deliverance. The old gentleman, a French Syrian, told me that when, three years before, he had heard of the coming of German troops to Sidon, he gave out to his neighbours that he and his family were going to the north, leaving the empty house in charge of the native caretaker. The family disappeared, and until the hurried departure of the Germans nothing more was seen of them, when they—apparently—returned once more to their home.

In reality, they had never left it. They had retired to a disused wing of the house, barricaded themselves in so skilfully that no one but the old caretaker who looked after the supplies suspected their presence; and there they had lived for three years, never venturing out except to walk at night in their extensive garden! On one occasion the house was occupied by a German staff-officer, and their walks ceased for three weeks; but for the greater part of the time it had remained untenanted. During the period previous to our coming they had been almost entirely without food, other than fruit and dried legumes.

That was the story told to me as nearly as I can remember it, and the lifeless pallor of the old Frenchman's face and those of his family certainly gave colour to the narrative. It is very hard to believe in starvation when you are surrounded on all sides by beautiful gardens and orchards abounding in fruit; and those at Sidon were surely the loveliest on earth. All round the town stretched great masses of green, in the midst of which, like diamonds in a sea of emeralds, were white cupolas and summer-houses, with scores of fountains playing all day long. On the hills behind the gardens were many modern houses admirably built after the Italian fashion, whose mellow terra-cotta blended effectively with the green mass below. Riding through the umbrageous lanes between countless orchards you could believe anything but that people here were starving.

The division had been promised a rest at Sidon for the remainder of the day, but shortly after two o'clock in the afternoon an urgent message came ordering us to make a forced march in order to reach Beyrout, thirty-five miles away, the following night! At four o'clock we left the beach and climbed steadily past those glorious gardens, until we struck the highroad. A few miles outside Sidon, we passed an inn which could not have changed much in character since the time of Christ. It formed a bridge across the road, and thus gave shelter to the passer-by from the noonday heat in summer and the torrential rains in winter; on one side there were the living rooms for the traveller and on the other side the stables wherein his ass or his horse could rest for the night. There were a few men lying in the shade of the "bridge" as we passed, and, peering into the stable, I could just see a donkey contentedly munching at the manger: the whole scene seemed to have come straight out of the New Testament.

Later in the afternoon I noticed a beautiful little house standing in its own garden, and rode over to examine it more closely. One thing only I saw; the rest was blotted out. Nailed to his door was the body of the owner, and beneath lay the charred—yes, charred—remains of what had once been his legs. He had been crucified and burnt alive; the twisted body, and the awful, tortured expression on the martyred man's face, left no room for doubt.

After a halt for a couple of hours at midnight we began the final stage. While it was yet dark we had tremendous difficulty with those camel-drivers who were unable to see at night, the *"mush-shuf-bi' leil's"* ("can't see-at-nights") we used to call them; and as we had a few blind camels as well the situation called for some ingenuity. The only way to solve the problem was to tie the men's wrists to the saddles of the camel immediately in front of them. They then allowed themselves to be towed along, keeping the rope just taut enough to act as a guide.

The blind camels were similarly treated, though even then there were accidents. One came shortly before dawn as we were crossing a viaduct with neither wall nor protection of any kind against a thirty-foot drop. A blind camel blundered towards the edge, slipped, and crashed down into the river-bed, and as he had 200 lbs. of biscuits on his back to speed his fall, it looked like a certain casualty. With some difficulty we clambered down to him, and found him not only alive but calmly grazing on the herbage around! And when the biscuits were removed he got up, grunting and snarling, but absolutely uninjured and ready to carry his load again.

As we approached Beyrout the signs of distress among the people grew more and more pronounced. Along the route were several tiny villages whose inhabitants gathered by the roadside to beg for food, and it was awful to see the wolfish way they ate the biscuits we gave them. At many places women stood with jars of water which they offered to the camel-drivers, not, I am sure, as a quid pro quo, but because it was all they had to offer.

Just at the entrance to the olive-groves, which extend for six miles out of Beyrout, I saw a dead child lying by the road-side, and from that point the journey became a succession of heartrending sights. Gaunt, lean-faced men, women thin to the point of emaciation, and children whose wizened faces made them look like old men, lined the route weeping for joy at their deliverance. Every one of our men as he passed handed over his day's rations of bully-beef and biscuits to the starving people; I saw one woman hysterically trying to insert a piece of army biscuit into the mouth of the baby in her arms, and groups of little boys fighting for the food thrown to them. It was pitiful to see the gratitude of people who succeeded in catching a biscuit or a tin of bully; and the way they welcomed our camel-drivers, who, of course, spoke Arabic like themselves, was a revelation.

A man, haggard with want, came out of his little wine-

shop and offered me a glass of aniseed, apologising courteously for its poor quality, and explaining that it was the only
drink he had been able to obtain for sale during the War!
A glance at the rows of empty bottles in his shop-window
confirmed the statement. God knows how he had earned his
living during the past three years. Towards evening the head
of the long column entered Beyrout: from miles behind on
the hills we could see the swinging kilts of the Highlanders,
while the sound of the bag-pipes floated faintly back to us. By
eight o'clock, we, too, were marching into the town through
crowds of delirious people, who clung to the troops as they
passed and kissed the boots of the mounted men; it was the
most painful, pitiful experience of all. As we swung down the
hill towards the beach a man said: "You are just in time, mon-
sieur; in six days we should all have been dead."

That was the main thing: we had marched ninety-six miles
in six days, we were dog-tired after a last continuous trek of
eighteen hours, but—we were in time!

CHAPTER 22

Deserted Villages in Lebanon

Sixty thousand people died of starvation in Beyrout during the War, out of a total population of one hundred and eighty thousand. There is overwhelming proof that this was a part of the brutal policy of systematic extermination adopted by the Turko-Germans towards the weaker races of Syria and Palestine. When Beyrout was evacuated the enemy collected all the food they could lay hands on, including the recently garnered harvest; and what they were unable to carry away with them they dumped in the harbour rather than give it to the starving people. Four hundred tons of foodstuffs were wantonly destroyed in this manner; and as an example of callous and spiteful vengeance, towards a people whose chief fault apparently was that they were hungry, this would be hard to beat.

The mortality amongst children was appalling. You could not ride out of the town without seeing their dead bodies lying by the roadside, where they had dropped from the arms of mothers too weak to carry them, often enough themselves lying dead a few yards farther on. In the poorer quarters of the town, especially near the docks, the dreadful death-roll lengthened every day. The Turks had gone out of their way to destroy many of the houses, with the result that hundreds of people were wandering about, foodless, homeless, and utterly friendless. For the first few days most of our work was carried on in and around the docks, where crowds of women and children congregated daily in the hope of obtaining food. I saw one small boy walking in front of me with a curious, unsteady gait, and just as I drew level with him he pitched forward on to his face without a sound. He was stone-dead when I turned him over; and judging by the terrible emaciation of his body he had died of protracted starvation.

Until the food ships arrived the British Army fed most of the people; I use the word "most" advisedly, for even here there were fat profiteers who had made fortunes out of the War, and who cared nothing for the sufferings of others. The poorer inhabitants literally thronged the various camps in search of food, and with characteristic generosity the troops tried to feed them all! They gave away bully-beef and biscuits to those most in need, and, whenever possible, their tea and sugar rations also; it was painful to see the gratitude of the recipients.

Except amongst the very wealthy both tea and sugar had been literally unknown for four years. When we entered Beyrout the price of tea was four hundred *piastres* (£4 2s.) per lb.—and chemically-treated stuff at that; and sugar, which was all but unobtainable by anybody, cost three hundred *piastres* per lb.! Within a week of our arrival you could buy both commodities in the shops at about twenty *piastres* and five *piastres* per lb. respectively.

But distress and suffering were not confined to Beyrout alone. On the pleasant hills of Lebanon north of the town are numerous villages through which the Turks had swept like a plague. Here the policy had been not so much starvation as extermination: whole villages were stripped of their inhabitants, who had been forcibly carried away, the men to slavery or death; the women to something worse. You could ride through village after village without seeing a soul, save perhaps an old man who would tell you that he was keeping the keys of the houses for their owners—who would never return. It is impossible to describe the pall of desolation that hung over those silent villages, a desolation that seemed to be accentuated by the beauty of the surrounding country.

Upwards of a quarter of a million people were either deported or massacred by the Turks in the Lebanon hills alone; and only in the villages occupied by Circassians, whom the Turks themselves had subsidised, were there any signs of even moderate prosperity. These people, moreover, showed marked hostility towards our troops, and had to be suppressed.

When the 7th Division left Beyrout in the middle of October to march farther north to Tripoli the situation was considerably easier. Food ships had arrived, and arrangements had been made for regular supplies to be given to the people, though at first they needed medical aid rather than food, so weakened were they by long privation and want. The chief difficulty in the distribution of supplies was the shortage of labour, for the advance had been so rapid that it had quite outdistanced the administrative branches of the service. Half a dozen R.A.S.C. clerks and a small party of the Egyptian Labour Corps, assisted by the "Camels," toiled night and day at the docks: we were dock-labourers, stevedores, and transport all in one. The fact that Beyrout was the only real port in the whole country nearer than Port Said did not tend to relieve the strain, for the natural disadvantages of Jaffa as a port prevented its being utilised to the full, while Haifa, although it possesses a magnificent harbour, had not as yet enough accommodation for ships.

Our own men now began to feel the effects of the arduous campaign. The rainy season was imminent, and malaria and blackwater fever claimed their victims by the score. The troops who had spent the previous five months stewing in the hothouse atmosphere of the Jordan Valley suffered particularly heavily through malignant malaria, contracted during those months, which lay dormant while operations were actually in progress and appeared when men were run down and weakened by their tremendous exertions. The Australian Mounted Division, who had been the first to enter Damascus, were amongst the hardest hit by the disease, for the oldest city in the world is also one of the most unhealthy—or was, at all events during the time of our occupation.

The River Abana, which runs through the city, was choked with dead horses and Turks for ten days. Hundreds of Turks wandered about, nominally prisoners, but with no one to guard them; they were far more numerous than our own men; and as the Turks generally had little idea of sanitation and less of personal cleanliness they were extremely unpleasant people to have about the place.

There were no regrets at leaving Damascus, for though the odour of sanctity may hang over the venerable city, it is as naught compared with the other odours, of which it has a greater and more pungent variety than any city in the country.

With the capture of Beyrout and Damascus hostilities had not ended, although the greater part of the Turkish Army had ceased to exist. While the 7th Division were en route to Tripoli the cavalry were making a corresponding advance in the centre, despite the ravages caused in their ranks by malaria. Indeed, with cheerful indifference to the geographical, to say nothing of the other difficulties in the way, they proposed to ride as far as Constantinople; that, it was felt, would be the crowning point of a great ride! However, for the moment they contented themselves with occupying Homs, a town on the caravan route about a hundred miles north of Damascus. Then General Allenby ordered a further advance on Aleppo, the last stronghold of the Turks in the country; and on October 21st the 5th Cavalry Division with the armoured cars started on what was to be their last ride. It was a worthy effort: in five days they covered a hundred miles, entering the city on October 26th, preceded the day before by the troops of the King of the Hedjaz, who had driven all the Turks away during the night.

After the capture of Aleppo, Turkey, having no army left, threw up the sponge, much to the disgust of the Australian Mounted Division, who, having reached Homs, hoped to be in at the death. Still, since theirs had been the honour of entering Damascus, it was but fitting that the 5th Cavalry Division should be the first into Aleppo, for the exploits of the two forces had been almost parallel throughout the campaign.

Thus in forty days, in the course of which the army had advanced upwards of five hundred miles, Turkey had been brought to her knees, her armies had been completely destroyed, and a country that had suffered from centuries of misrule had been cleared of the oppressor. It is, however, significant of the bitter hatred the Turks bear towards the Armenians and other races of Asia Minor, that even after the Armistice one of the chief troubles of our troops was to prevent the Turkish prisoners, who were awaiting transportation to the great camps in Egypt, from maltreating Armenians wherever and whenever they came into contact with them! Drastic measures with Turkey will have to be adopted by the Allies if these little nations are to live in comfort and security in the future.

The weeks following the surrender of Turkey were occupied by the army in feeding the people, in reinstating them on the land, and in setting up a stable form of government in the country. It is unnecessary here to enter into detail, but it may be stated that the policy which had met with universal approval in Palestine was adopted in Syria. Subject to certain obvious limitations every man was free to come and go as he pleased; and, with no restriction whatever, he could worship as he pleased, whether Christian, Mussulman, or Jew. To quote one example of the goodwill that prevailed: the head of the Greek Church in Homs offered his Cathedral to the Army for the thanksgiving service held after the signing of the general Armistice, and members of nearly every religious denomination were present at a most impressive ceremony.

The Arabs took over the government of Damascus and the surrounding country, which presumably they will retain for the future; the French, who have large interests in Beyrout and Lebanon, will, I believe, be the paramount influence there—though curiously enough, the one question we were constantly asked by the people of Beyrout was whether the British were going to take over the town; and from fifteen miles north of Acre down to the Suez Canal the country will probably be under the protection of the British. As this includes the desert of Northern Sinai the conquest of which had taken two long years, it is unlikely that we shall be accused of land-grabbing!

It is reasonably certain that Palestine will need material help for some time, for Turkish maladministration, and the iniquitously heavy taxes imposed upon the people, have almost killed initiative. So far as real development is concerned, it is almost a virgin land, and although the efforts of those responsible for the work of reconstruction are both vigorous and successful, it will be many years before Palestine is producing up to her full capacity. At present the grain crop of the entire country could be brought to England in about seven ships; in fact, before the War most of it was bought by a well-known firm of whisky distillers!

Whether the Jews as a nation will ever settle in Palestine is a question the future alone will solve; certainly the wise policy of the British and French governments offers them every inducement, if they really wish to become a nation again in their own ancient land. If the prophets are to be believed Jerusalem will one day be the capital of the world—but it will not be in our day.

LEONAUR

ALSO FROM LEONAUR
AVAILABLE IN SOFTCOVER OR HARDCOVER WITH DUST JACKET

DOING OUR 'BIT' *by Ian Hay*—Two Classic Accounts of the Men of Kitchener's 'New Army' During the Great War including *The First 100,000 & All In It.*

AN EYE IN THE STORM by *Arthur Ruhl*—An American War Correspondent's Experiences of the First World War from the Western Front to Gallipoli and Beyond.

STAND & FALL by *Joe Cassells*—A Soldier's Recollections of the 'Contemptible Little Army' and the Retreat from Mons to the Marne, 1914.

RIFLEMAN MACGILL'S WAR by *Patrick MacGill*—A Soldier of the London Irish During the Great War in Europe including *The Amateur Army, The Red Horizon & The Great Push.*

WITH THE GUNS by *C. A. Rose & Hugh Dalton*—Two First Hand Accounts of British Gunners at War in Europe During World War 1- Three Years in France with the Guns and With the British Guns in Italy.

EAGLES OVER THE TRENCHES by *James R. McConnell & William B. Perry*—Two First Hand Accounts of the American Escadrille at War in the Air During World War 1-Flying For France: With the American Escadrille at Verdun and Our Pilots in the Air.

THE BUSH WAR DOCTOR by *Robert V. Dolbey*—The Experiences of a British Army Doctor During the East African Campaign of the First World War.

THE 9TH—THE KING'S (LIVERPOOL REGIMENT) IN THE GREAT WAR 1914 - 1918 by *Enos H. G. Roberts*—Like many large cities, Liverpool raised a number of battalions in the Great War. Notable among them were the Pals, the Liverpool Irish and Scottish, but this book concerns the wartime history of the 9th Battalion – The Kings.

THE GAMBARDIER by *Mark Severn*—The experiences of a battery of Heavy artillery on the Western Front during the First World War.

FROM MESSINES TO THIRD YPRES by *Thomas Floyd*—A personal account of the First World War on the Western front by a 2/5th Lancashire Fusilier.

THE IRISH GUARDS IN THE GREAT WAR - VOLUME 1 by *Rudyard Kipling*—Edited and Compiled from Their Diaries and Papers Volume 1 The First Battalion.

THE IRISH GUARDS IN THE GREAT WAR - VOLUME 2 by *Rudyard Kipling*—Edited and Compiled from Their Diaries and Papers Volume 2 The Second Battalion.

Lightning Source UK Ltd.
Milton Keynes UK
170903UK00001B/42/A